UNSHAKABLE

Establishing The Foundations of Faith

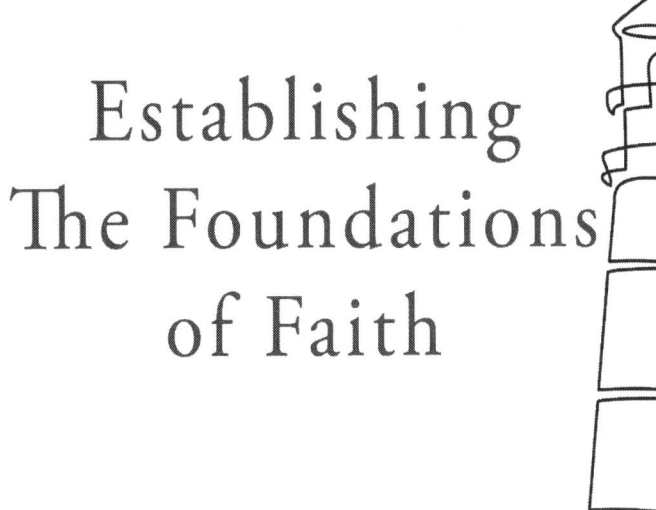

NATHAN TANNER
with
DR. JIM RICHARDS

Copyright © 2023 Nathan Tanner and Dr. Jim Richards All rights reserved.

No part of this publication may be reproduced, stored, or transmitted in any form or by any means, including written, copied, or electronically, without prior written permission from the author or his agents. The only exception is brief quotations in printed reviews. Short excerpts may be used with the publisher's or author's expressed written permission.

All Scripture quotations, unless otherwise noted, are from the New King James Version of the Bible. Copyright © 1982 by Thomas Nelson, Inc. Used by permission. All rights reserved.

Unshakable: Establishing The Foundations Of Faith

Cover and Interior Page design by True Potential, Inc.

ISBN: (Paperback): 9781960024237

ISBN: (e-book): 9781960024244

LCCN: 2023947614

True Potential, Inc.

PO Box 904, Travelers Rest, SC 29690

www.truepotentialmedia.com

Produced and Printed in the United States of America.

Contents

Introduction: Searching For Life	5
Section 1. Building on the Rock	11
Introduction	13
1. Becoming a Disciple	15
2. Christ Our Cornerstone	21
3. Redemption Accomplished	27
Section 2 Faith-Righteousness	33
Introduction	35
4. The Power of Faith-Righteousness	41
5. Whose Righteousness?	47
6. The Stumbling Stone of the Gospel	51
Section 3 Repentance from Dead Works.	57
Introduction	59
7. Defining Repentance	63
8. Motive Changes Everything	67
9. The Empowerment of Grace	73
Section 4 Faith in God	77
Introduction	79
10. The Secret to Steadfast Faith	83
11. The Gospel of Peace	89
12. Jesus, Our Substitute	93

Section 5. Teachings of Baptisms	**99**
Introduction	101
13. The Significance of Baptism.	105
14. Water Baptism	111
15. Baptism into the Holy Spirit	115
Section 6 Laying On Of Hands	**121**
Introduction	123
16. Laying on of Hands in Scripture	125
17. Ministering in Power	131
18. Releasing Your Faith	137
Section 7 Resurrection From The Dead	**141**
Introduction	143
19. The Centrality of the Resurrection	145
20. A Future Resurrection	151
21. Eternal Life Now	155
Section 8 Eternal Judgment	**159**
Introduction	161
22. Judgment Future	165
23. Judgment Past	171
24. The Judgment Seat of Christ	175
Section 9 Experiencing Transformation	**181**
25. The Goal of the Gospel	183
26. Heaven on Earth	187
27. Conditioning Your Heart	191
28. Putting on the New	197
Conclusion Making the Journey	**201**

Introduction: Searching For Life

Dr. Jim Richards

People from different cultures use different terminology to explain what they seek when they come to Jesus! Regardless of the wording, the search for God is usually a quest for a better quality of life. When I came to Jesus, I didn't know any religious terminology. Instead, I expressed my heart in words I understood! My words were a reflection of my desperate cry for help!

While few people can adequately express the sense of lack that they feel when God is not their life source, the sense of something missing from their life is ever-present. As believers, we know that the missing element is the life of God. Jesus said, explicitly clarifying his goal for the human race, *"I have come that they may have life, and that they may have it more abundantly."* (John 10:10 NKJV)

The life to which Jesus refers comes from the Greek word "zoe." Unfortunately, "zoe" is nearly always translated as eternal life, which is a nonsensical translation. When we leave this realm, we leave the dimension of time. Eternity exists in the absence of time. Since there is no time in eternity, we must consider a more meaningful translation of the word.

Some of the best Greek language tools translate "zoe" as a quality of life,[1]

---

1   The state of one who is possessed of vitality or is animate from Thayer's Greek Lexicon, PC Study Bible formatted Electronic Database. Copyright © 2006 by Biblesoft, Inc. All rights reserved.

or the quality of life possessed by God.[2] Jesus came to bring us the quality of life possessed by God. Jesus was the exact representation of God. (Hebrews 1:3) He is the Word of God made flesh. (John 1:14) Everything God desires to reveal to us about himself is manifest in Jesus. Any view or opinion we have about God, any interpretation or application of the Word of God that is not based on the life, ministry, teaching, and covenant God made with Jesus, is not only incorrect but does not glorify God and actually opposes God!

Jesus is the center of all life. God chose to glorify himself through the Son. The life is in him; it emits from his being. Just as the physical universe was created by him and for him, our spiritual life is created by him and for him. He is the personification of the righteousness of God, the reality that sustains all life. Therefore, our pursuit must be for him personally, not just the life that he gives.

In creation, we have our first glimpse of righteousness and why it is so essential to our quality of life. Creation had one very specific goal, to provide a perfect quality of life for mankind. The universe, the galaxies, our solar system, and our physical bodies had to function in perfect harmony to provide optimal quality of life. All of the creation had to be aligned to precise specifications. Trillions of precise measurements, perfectly tuned frequencies, and every form of energy had to be synchronized with the billions of chemical and energetic functions of human cells that occur every minute of every day, or life on earth would have been an impossibility. All the stars and planets of all the galaxies had to be perfectly spaced, aligned, and coordinated to move in exact patterns; otherwise, life as we know it could not exist.

In the creation account, when God said, "Let there be...." The Hebrew word for "said" puts the emphasis on the fact that before speaking, God conceived the outcome in his heart, and he had a specific intention. Then after the creation, he inspected the outcome and said, "It is good!"

As far as we can understand, God's intention in creation was to bring about a perfect habitat for the human race to live, a perfect life with no death, sickness, disease, pain, or sorrow. Then, upon observing his work, he saw that each phase of creation was good. The word "good" has the

---

2   Herman Cremer, Biblico-Theological Lexicon of New Testament Greek, Edinburgh, 1895, p 272

Introduction: Searching For Life

very obvious meaning of desirable and pleasing. But the Hebrew word for good always embodies the concept of harmony. God's intention was a perfect creation, fully capable of sustaining life without death! We know God's outcome was in perfect harmony with his intentions, and his intention was life at its best! Because it fulfilled his intentions, he declared it good!

In our "spiritual lives," God has given us the information, power, and authority needed to keep ourselves in harmony with him, thereby experiencing the best quality of life possible in this realm. Just like the physical creation, the degree to which we harmonize our lives with God, we will experience the quality of life possessed by Jesus. I am not talking about earning that life; I am talking about harmonizing with something that we have because we are in Jesus and because he is the life!

> **THE DEGREE TO WHICH WE HARMONIZE OUR LIVES WITH GOD, WE WILL EXPERIENCE THE QUALITY OF LIFE POSSESSED BY JESUS.**

There was perfect life and no death on planet Earth until man brought about one change! Man wanted to determine good and evil independently of God. Since the word "good" is a desirable, pleasing state that comes from being in harmony with God, we see that the word "evil" is an undesirable state resulting from disharmony with God. Just as harmony aligns us with life, disharmony aligns us with death.

A perfect creation sustained life with no death for one reason; it was in perfect harmony with God and his intentions. Death entered in for one reason; man brought disharmony with God into creation. It could no longer sustain his intentions. The innumerable factors that had to be in perfect harmony to sustain life had been disrupted by man's choices.

The disharmony introduced by mankind began in ways that didn't totally collapse creation, but it did introduce pain, destruction, and death by degrees. Originally, humans lived forever. But after they rebelled and demanded the right to determine good and evil, death entered. Death didn't enter as punishment from God; death entered because man chose to seek fulfillment in those things that were out of harmony with how God created us.

Part of the deception of sin was probably the fact that they didn't fall over dead the moment they introduced sin into the equation. Over time, little by little, their life span decreased to a little less than a thousand years, to a little over one hundred years, and today about 70-80 years, most of which are plagued with sickness and infirmity. To the degree that the human race has entered into disharmony with God, death in all its degrees and aspects has increased. Despite the propaganda of the anti-God establishment, the human experience hasn't progressively gotten better and better; it has gotten worse and worse!

This history of disharmony and its effects on the physical world is a clear model of disharmony that also occurs on the emotional and spiritual plains! In the physical model, we can understand the continuum of sin and death. We can finally understand that death is not a penalty initiated by God. It is the end result of choices. In the beginning, creation existed in righteousness; God's definitions of good and evil were observed. Then mankind introduced unrighteousness by defining good and evil for himself, unrighteousness prevailed, and death came, but what does that mean?

The word "righteous," at its most basic level, means "right." God is righteous, i.e., he is right. What is he right about? He is right about everything, but primarily about good and evil. He is also right about the fact that when we disrupt harmony with God, death and destruction follow. Religion will always try to make you believe that consequences are the judgment of God, but the Scripture reveals that when we choose a specific way of life, we also choose the consequences.

Just as harmony in the physical creation sustained life, harmony in the emotional and spiritual realm also requires harmony to sustain life (zoe). To the degree that we depart from God's truth, we introduce disharmony, destruction, and ultimately death. God's righteousness is the only way to maintain harmony and life. All his "rules" for life and peace are right, i.e., they work. His intention with truth is so we can know how to have life at its best. His warnings are not the threats of an angry, vindictive deity. They are the attempts of a loving Father to prevent or rescue his children from suffering.

We tend to think of sin as something we do that displeases God, for which he punishes us in an attempt to bring us back in line! But sin is

Introduction: Searching For Life

actually that which introduces death into our existence. His displeasure is in the pain introduced into our lives by unrighteousness.

Sin is that which deviates from the glory of God. That which glorifies God is that which fulfills his intention of abundant life. Thus, anything out of harmony with what God has declared to be good will produce death. All it takes for creation to lose its harmony with God's perfect intention is any degree of imperfection, i.e., a departure from what he declares to be perfect. Righteousness is like the tuning of a piano. All the strings need not be out of tune for it to sound bad, nor does it have to be extremely out of tune. One string slightly out of tune affects its overall sound quality because it is out of harmony with itself and all the other instruments in the orchestra.

In the physical world, with a slight deviation in the magnetic flux of the earth, a change in gravity, or any of the other energetic factors, quality of life begins to diminish. The same is true when it comes to sin. Minor discrepancies in spiritual factors create an imbalance that can bring about imperceivable variations resulting in monumental degrees of destruction.

The precision balance of creation is a manifestation of physical righteousness. (Romans 1:20) Likewise, the perfection of every word and deed is an expression of righteousness. No one has the knowledge, capacity, or inherent righteousness to recognize and maintain all the factors required to stand before God as righteous. Nor does anyone have the sensitivity to recognize and deal with all the times we deviate from perfect harmony with God! Consequently, in his great love, God provided righteousness in Christ Jesus, which can be accessed by faith in his death, burial, and resurrection.

> **THE PRECISION BALANCE OF CREATION IS A MANIFESTATION OF PHYSICAL RIGHTEOUSNESS.**

So, we know God wants us to have "zoe" (eternal life), but it is unattainable by our own means. Fortunately, He doesn't leave us in the dark, attempting to figure out who he is and what he wants. God has gone to great lengths to reveal himself and his process toward life. *And this is eternal life, that they may know You, the only true God, and Jesus Christ whom You have sent.* (John 17:3 NKJV)

The only way to know (experience) God is to know (experience) Jesus. The foundational doctrines in this book will teach you about Jesus; should you choose to accept his truth fully by surrendering to him as Lord, you will move beyond knowing the information to know the One of Whom the information speaks. By harmonizing your life with him, you will harmonize with God, the Father. You will see and know God as he is to the degree that you are willing to see and know Jesus as he is.

Just as Jesus upholds the perfect harmony of all the innumerable factors of creation by the *word of his power* (Hebrews 1:3b), likewise, he upholds millions of factors involved in "zoe" (Life of God) by the power of his righteousness. In him, we see God, know God, understand God, and experience God. But more importantly, in him, we qualify for the inheritance in his Kingdom. (Colossians 1:12-14)

Knowing him (experientially) and taking his yoke, i.e., harmonizing with him, we harmonize with God. We experience the righteousness of God that is beyond human comprehension and certainly beyond human capacity to earn or maintain. The writer of Hebrews tells us this righteousness is the pathway to perfection, i.e., maturity and stability.

In this book, you will discover the seven doctrines of the New Covenant, which provide the basis for life as an overcomer. As these truths unfold in your heart, you can experience God in ways few modern believers have known. You will avoid the struggles, traps, and failures common to so many. You will find the life you desire when you set out on this journey with Jesus!

Section 1. Building on the Rock

For additional information and to locate the resources mentioned in this book please visit:

https://www.truepotentialmedia.com/unshakable/

or use your smartphone camera to open the link in the QR Code below.

Introduction

Dr. Jim Richards

When administering a "polygraph test," one must identify the truth before being able to recognize a lie. This is done by asking a few questions to which the one analyzing the results knows the correct answer. Is your name Bob? If the person's name is Bob and they reply in the affirmative, the graph will provide a specific pattern. This is called establishing a baseline. Once a baseline is established, every response is compared to the graph of the baseline question's answer to determine if the response is true or false.

When negotiating or questioning anyone, if we have a baseline of what we know to be absolutely true, we simply compare all the other responses with the baseline answers. If the answers are congruent with the baseline, they are probably true. This is a tactic used by interrogators to catch people lying.

God has provided the believer with His baseline truth. Everything else we read in the Scriptures can be compared to the baseline truth to provide us with the certainty of whether or not we are correctly interpreting what we read. This baseline of truth forms a foundation. The foundation supports and sustains all that is built on it!

The universe was created based on a particular foundation. Sin (deviation from that which glorifies God) has been eroding that foundation since man introduced it. Apart from an intervention that the Bible calls the Second Coming, a time would come when our planet would completely implode. All things that exist in the created realm are built on this eroding foundation. When that foundation crumbles, whatever is built on it will collapse.

The writer of the Book of Hebrews identified a foundation for New Covenant Faith. These seven doctrines provide the basis for faith that is unshakable and immovable. They also provide a spiritual GPS that ensures we will never "run off the rails" with strange doctrine. Furthermore, it provides a path to ensure that we grow to be spiritually mature believers who can not only stand strong for ourselves but can also become teachers and leaders that guard and guide the flock of God! These seven doctrines comprise a shield of truth that will guard our hearts and minds against spiritual deception.

When teaching about the importance of a good foundation, Jesus used the example of building our house on the rock or on the sand. In Hebrew, the letter for heart and house is the BET. Just as the house is a place of safety, nurturing, and love for the family, the heart is the seat of all we are spiritually and emotionally. His teaching depicts, among other things, how one's heart can be brought to ruin if its beliefs are not built on the foundation of Jesus' logos (words). Conversely, it reveals that a house built on the rock of his teaching will endure the storms of life, preventing the downfall of the house (heart).

The foundation is the most crucial part of a structure. No matter how good the material or the quality of craftsmanship, a building is only as stable as its foundation. Without the foundation provided by God's Word, we will be unstable, ill-equipped to help others, and run the risk of our lives becoming totally unmanageable.

When Jesus warned of the refusal to build on his "sayings," he used the word "logos." The logos is more than information or intellectual truth. It is far beyond the intellectual definitions of words written on a page. It is the word inspired by God, written on our hearts, mixed with faith, and empowered for application by the grace of God.

As you read the following pages, I would encourage you to use the seven doctrines to evaluate your current beliefs about God. Any place you find a discrepancy between the foundations of the faith and your current beliefs, make the proper adjustments.

1. Becoming a Disciple

Throughout the course of this book, we are going to be talking about building an unshakable foundation in your walk with God. The unfortunate thing for many Christians is that they build their Christian life on a shakable and faulty foundation. As they continue in their relationship with God, they're disappointed to see that the promises of God are not working in their daily lives.

Over the course of this book, if you take the time to not just accumulate knowledge and information, but to establish your heart in the truth of the New Covenant foundations of faith, your entire Christian life will be different. It will greatly improve, and you're going to see the promises of God working in your life. You're also going to see the fulfillment of the things that you desire from the Lord. Apart from the New Birth, which is the most important thing, the greatest investment you can make in your life is to establish yourself in these foundational truths of the Gospel.

T.L. Osborne used to say, "If what you are teaching cannot be translated under a banana tree in Africa, then you're over-complicating it." Most of us want wisdom, we want to appear important, and we want to know all the information, but we don't have the truth of the simple Gospel working in our lives.

Hebrews chapter 5:12-6:3 is a key scripture passage that we're going to keep going back to in this book; I would encourage you to read the passage in several different translations and to familiarize yourself with what the author of Hebrews is trying to communicate.

The Bible tells us, in Hebrews, chapter 6, about six foundational doctrines that we need to grasp and interpret through the lens of faith-righteousness.

In the next section, we are going to look at faith-righteousness. I can assure you that it is probably very different from what you've originally been taught. Faith-righteousness is the cornerstone and capstone that ties all these foundational pieces together.

Hebrews 5:12 says, *"For though by this time you ought to be teachers, you need someone to teach you again the first principles of the oracles of God; and You have come to need milk and not solid food." (NKJV)*

Let me ask you this: why do people have to be retaught so often? The author says that by this time, you should be teachers. You should be the ones that are teaching people the Word of God, but you need someone else to teach you again the basics or foundations of the Gospel.

> **WE SHOULD NEVER WONDER WHERE GOD IS IN ANY GIVEN SITUATION.**

No one who really takes the time to lay this foundation will ever be confused—either in life or in doctrine. We should never wonder where God is in any given situation. We should never wonder if he has abandoned us or think that he has let us down. We should not question whether or not we could have sinned away our salvation. If you take the time to lay this foundation, you are never going to be troubled by questions that plague most Christians, usually throughout their entire lives.

Hebrews goes on to say, *"For everyone who partakes only of milk is unskilled in the word of righteousness, for he is a babe."* A baby is someone who is unskilled or unlearned in the word of righteousness. Scripture continues, *"But solid food belongs to those who are of full age, that is, those who by reason of use have their senses exercised to discern both good and evil."*

What does the author mean by *"reason of use"*? That's an old English way of saying, put it into practice. What he's saying is that if you take the time to build this foundation and apply the truth, you're not a baby. You are mature. It's because you have learned how to apply the Word of God, not just know information, but actually how to apply it to your life.

Again, he goes on to say, *"those who by reason of use have their senses exercised to discern both good and evil."* I don't believe that he's just talking about good and evil in the sense of right and wrong. It doesn't take a mature person of God to know right from wrong. What he is saying is that it takes a mature person to discern truth from error with regard to Gospel truth.

Over the course of this book, you're going to learn how to discern what is right and what is Gospel truth. You may discover that much of what you have built your relationship with God upon is actually based on a faulty foundation.

Does the truth always work?

My question for you is, "Does the truth always work"? The normal answer for Christians is that absolutely, the truth always works. Let's see what Jesus said about truth in John 8:31- 32 in the Amplified Bible:

"Jesus said to those Jews who had believed on him" (notice that these are people that believed that Jesus was the son of God, the Messiah), *"If you abide in my word, hold fast to my teaching and live in accordance with them, you are truly my disciples, and you will know the truth and the truth will set you free."*

So, to answer the question, it is only the truth that is applied to your life and that you know by experience and have allowed to change your heart that will set you free.

Jesus said, *"If you abide in my word…"* Abide is a key word here. *"If you abide… then you will know the truth and the truth will set you free."* Most of us know the truth. We have an intellectual understanding of the truth, but it's not working in our lives because we haven't committed ourselves to the process of discipleship. Discipleship is the process of allowing the Word of God to change our thoughts, our opinions, and the way that we see life. It is a daily and lifelong commitment.

If you want to be a disciple, it is the road of repentance. It's the road of consistently and daily allowing the Word of God to change and shape the way you see things. Until you actually commit yourself to a life of discipleship and allowing the Word of God to change you and your perception, you're just playing religion. In that condition, you're not going to see the power of the Word of God working in your life.

We must know the truth. The biblical word for 'know' means that we know something or someone through personal experience. When the Bible talks about knowledge, it's not talking about just accumulating information. It's talking about knowledge that is taken and applied to our lives.

This process of surrendering our view and opinion for God's is also called repentance. The biblical idea of repentance is a change of thinking and believing that, in turn, redirects the course of our entire life.

Often, we know about these things, but we're not willing to take the next step to commit our lives to them. Through this investment of time and study that you are taking in your life and heart, you are committing to beginning the journey that allows these truths to shape the way you see God, the world, and yourself.

How is that working for you?

Many of the doctrines that we have do not work because we don't have a foundation to support them. We haven't taken the time to establish our lives on the proper foundation. All we have is doctrine.

When there's a conflict between the pain that we feel in our body and the promises of God for healing and wholeness, it is difficult for a person to walk out their healing. What gives us the foundation to stand on until the promise becomes a reality? It's this foundation that we are talking about! It will give you the foundation and the support to walk out your healing.

What about provision? The Bible makes incredible promises for God's provision, prosperity, and financial blessing. What foundation are you going to stand on until you actually begin to walk out these promises in your life? The promises are there. The promises are neutral. Though they are available to all, most of us don't have a foundation to support those promises until we actually see them working in our lives.

The foundation makes your future sure. It gives you a place to stand until the promises become a reality. The problem is not with the promises; the problem is with our belief system. It's that we don't have a correct foundation to support the promises until we begin to see them walked out in our daily lives.

Surefooted in the Gospel of Peace

In Ephesians 6:15, the Bible says that we are to *"shod our feet with the preparation of the gospel of peace."* What is significant here is that Paul is saying that our footing and our standing are to be on the Gospel of peace. If one went into battle, especially during the time of the Roman Empire, the most important thing about the tactical battle gear worn was what was worn on the feet- the shoes.

The Romans would outfit the soles of their soldiers' shoes with tiny spikes or cleats. This would give them a sure footing on the battlefield. When you are on a slippery slope and you drop on the battlefield, you don't want the enemy upon you as you regain your footing.

Paul is comparing the believers' fight to the Roman battlefield. Later in this book, we are going to look in detail at the Gospel of Peace, but for now, we need to understand our need for a firm foundation that comes from the readiness of mind in the Gospel of Peace.

Ask yourself, can I stand on my beliefs when all else fails? When your body says one thing, and your beliefs another? When your body says, I'm sick, I'm dying, do you have a foundation to support the promise of healing? Do you have a foundation to stand on when your own heart condemns you and tells you God does not love you? Or when you look at your life and say, my life does not line up with the life that I know God created me to live? It's then that condemnation can come in and say, you're a fake, you're a hypocrite, God doesn't love you. You're going to keep making the same mistakes. A correct foundation will give you the support to stand until the promises of God begin to work out in your life.

> ASK YOURSELF, CAN I STAND ON MY BELIEFS WHEN ALL ELSE FAILS?

Chapter Questions

1. Honestly evaluate your life and ask yourself if you are totally committed to the life of a disciple. Before going any further, take some time to surrender your life to Jesus as your Lord and then set your intention to follow him as a disciple.

2. Will the truth automatically change your life? What did Jesus say about this in John 8:31-32?

3. What does it mean to you to have a solid foundation in your relationship with God and your understanding of the truth?

2. Christ Our Cornerstone

Proverbs 10:25 NKJV says, *"When the whirlwind passes by, the wicked are no more, but the righteous has an everlasting foundation."* In the Hebrew language, wicked does not just mean evil. The word could and should often be translated as "crooked." Also, when it says righteous, the word could have been simply translated as "straight."

When your heart is not straight, it is crooked, perhaps not in a moral sense, but crooked in the way that you see God. When your heart is crooked, you will not see things as they are but as your crooked perception suggests. Whirlwinds will come, storms will come, and if you're not steadfast in the truth of the gospel, you are going to get washed away.

The righteous or the straight has an everlasting foundation. The person whose heart and beliefs are in line with the truth of the New Covenant has a firm footing. An everlasting foundation will give us the footing upon which we stand. It gives us the basis for all future support and also gives us the basis for all future provision.

Psalms 11:3 NKJV says, *"If the foundations are destroyed, what can the righteous do?"* The answer is to take the time to lay the foundation. If you are righteous, you are righteous through the blood of Jesus Christ. It's not something that you've earned or deserved. It's something that's been given to you.

Do we really trust Jesus?

You may need to ask yourself if Jesus is really your foundation. You might need to take the time to go to God and ask the hard questions. The right

Christian answer is yes! Of course, Jesus is my foundation! But when push comes to shove, it is often not the reality in many of our lives. Jesus is often not our foundation in the practical everyday sense. We often hold to the historical or the religious Jesus, but not the Jesus of the New Testament, the one who is Lord overall.

Is Jesus your Lord, and are you his disciple? Many of us want the benefits of the Kingdom without surrendering our views and opinions. Jesus said it like this, *"Repent for the Kingdom of heaven is at hand."* We talk about the Kingdom of God, and through the New Birth, we have access to the Kingdom of God, but we only experience the Kingdom of God through a daily lifestyle of repentance.

Christ our cornerstone

When I was a young man, I apprenticed under a stone mason and began to learn the trade. Now, when the Bible talks about the cornerstone of the house being Jesus Christ, I go back to my stone masonry days.

When we were building a stone or a block wall, it was absolutely essential that the first stones were straight and level because they determined the course of the whole building. We took extra care to lay that cornerstone precisely and accurately because everything after that was to be built upon it and find direction from it. All the other stones would be set in reference to this stone, thus determining the position of the entire structure.

> ARE WE TRUSTING JESUS? OR ARE WE JUST TRUSTING OUR DOCTRINES?

If Jesus is our rock, then he is our cornerstone. He's the one that we build upon, the one providing stability, safety, and security. We need not only the right information but the grace to apply the truth to our hearts and to our lives.

Are we trusting Jesus? Or are we just trusting our doctrines? Let's test ourselves. One way to determine what you really believe in any given situation is to check your first response or default beliefs. When you get sick, do you go back to the Book of Job and wonder if maybe God had a hand in it, or do you look to Christ and his perfect work on the Cross?

Job blamed God because that was his default belief. We blame God if that is our default belief. Many believe that God is controlling everything and, therefore, what happens must be God's will. That was Job's default. However, later in the book, he declares, *"For the thing which I greatly feared has come upon me."* (Job 3:25 KJV) His fears came upon him, not the will of God.

I Corinthians 3:11 NKJV says, *"For no other foundation, can anyone lay than that which is laid, which is Jesus Christ."*

Mentally we agree with that, but when we get into a tight spot, when push comes to shove, we see that Jesus is really not our foundation.

Jesus gave a parable in Luke 6:46-49 NKJV:

> *But why do you call me Lord, Lord, and do not do the things which I say? Whoever comes to me, and hears my sayings and does them, I will show you whom he is like- he is like a man building a house who dug deep and laid the foundation on the rock. And when the flood arose, the stream beat vehemently against that house and could not shake it, for it was founded on the rock. But he who heard it and did nothing- he is like a man who built a house on the earth without a foundation, against which the stream beat vehemently and immediately it fell. And the ruin of that house was great.*

Again, Jesus is saying, "Don't come to me and say, 'Lord, Lord,' if you're not going to apply the things that I am teaching you, and if you're not going to take the time to lay this foundation." He then tells them a story about a man who took the time to lay that foundation, investing in his life and future.

I've laid foundations. I've built houses, and the foundation is the part of the house that we don't pay attention to. It's the part of the house that doesn't stand out. Yet it's the part of the house that, if neglected and done wrong, will give you major problems later on. If the foundation is off, sooner or later, you're going to find other areas that are wrong with the house.

Jesus says the wise man is someone who builds on the right foundation. The storms of this life are going to come. They come on the righteous and the sinner. Life is not fair. Just because you're a believer in Jesus

Christ doesn't mean you're exempt from the storms of life. They will come. The difference is that if you take the time to build correctly, you will have a foundation to ride out the storm. You will be the one that is still standing, still prospering, and still walking out the promises of God long after the storm has passed.

Paul, the apostle, was a foundation layer. In 1 Corinthians 3:10 -11 NKJV, He explains, "I have laid the foundation, and now another builds on it." Next, he says, *"For no other foundation can anyone lay than that which is laid, which is Jesus Christ."* Paul understood that for there to be an effective, growing church and an effective, growing disciple of Jesus Christ, there must be this one foundation.

Ephesians 2:19-21 NKJV says:

> *Now, therefore, you are no longer strangers and foreigners, but fellow citizens with the saints and members of the household of God, having been built on the foundation of the apostles and prophets, Jesus Christ himself being the chief cornerstone, in whom the whole building fitted together, grows into a holy temple in the Lord.*

We may build on the foundation of the apostles and prophets, but the cornerstone must be Jesus Christ. As leaders and ministers, our call is not to straighten people out or convince them to live right, or persuade them to serve our vision. Our call is to establish people on the rock.

Teachers or infants?

Let's go back to Hebrews 5:12 NKJV. The author says, *"For though by this time you ought to be teachers, you need someone to teach you again the first principles of the oracles of God; and you have come to need milk and not solid food."*

And then he says in Hebrews 6:1-2:

> *Therefore, leaving the discussion of the elementary principles of Christ, let us go on to perfection, not laying again the foundation of repentance from dead works, but of faith toward God, of the doctrine of baptisms, of laying on of hands, of resurrection of the dead, and of eternal judgment.*

He says, "Let's not lay again this foundation." And then he gives us six foundation stones. Now, when he says not laying again, he's not saying that we never need to go back to these fundamental truths. That's likely not what the apostle had in mind when he said, "Don't lay it again." What he means is for us to lay this foundation and then start building on it. If you take the time to lay it, you're not going to have to continue laying that same foundation over and over again. You will instead have a solid foundation to build upon.

Another way we can look at it is that "don't lay it again" could also be translated as "don't cast down" this foundation. Don't let someone come along with a new fad or a new teaching that causes you to break down this foundation. It's the foundation, and it's stable. Build it up, get it right, don't abandon it. Hold onto it no matter what!

These six foundational doctrines are what we are to build upon. This is one of the clearest passages in scripture. It actually lays out the specifics of those foundational doctrines. There's a reason that they put this in the word of God so clearly. Next, he gives us the key to interpreting all of the doctrines. The key is faith-righteousness, built on the cornerstone of Jesus Christ himself. Therefore Jesus, through his finished work, is the cornerstone.

In 1 Corinthians 2:1-5 NKJV, Paul says:

> *And I, brethren, when I came to you, did not come with excellence of speech or of wisdom declaring to you the testimony of God. For I determined not to know anything among you except Jesus Christ and Him crucified. I was with you in weakness, in fear, and in much trembling. And my speech and my preaching were not with persuasive words of human wisdom, but in demonstration of the Spirit and of power, that your faith should not be in the wisdom of men but in the power of God.*

The apostle says that when he came to them, when he brought the Gospel, he did not come with excellence of speech and wisdom. He told them that his message and his preaching were simple. That he determined to know nothing while he was with them except Jesus Christ and him crucified.

I don't think that the apostle was saying that the only thing he preached was a born-again experience. Why? He also led the Corinthians into the baptism of the Holy Spirit and taught so much more. I believe that what he was saying is that everything else that he taught was on the foundation of Jesus Christ and him crucified. He was saying:

> *For I determined not to know anything among you except Jesus Christ and Him crucified. I was with you in weakness, in fear, and in much trembling. And my speech and my preaching were not with persuasive words of human wisdom, but in demonstration of the Spirit and of power.*

The people of Corinth had their lives transformed. They not only saw the miracles, but because the foundation was Jesus Christ and his finished work, their lives were transformed and built on a solid foundation.

Chapter Questions

1. Do you struggle to receive the promises of God? Why do you think that is the situation?

2. If Jesus is the cornerstone of all truth, how should you approach any doctrine or teaching that seems to contradict how Jesus lived, taught, and what he accomplished in the New Covenant?

3. Redemption Accomplished

What Jesus accomplished on the Cross, and the steps that he took to complete our redemption, provide a basis that we can constantly use as a reference. From these, we are to evaluate what we believe and determine if what we believe is based on the truth of Christ's finished work. We need to ask ourselves if what we believe is in line with what Jesus Christ accomplished or if it is just a religious tradition.

Through his teaching and ministry, and then through his death, burial, and resurrection, Jesus completed the work of redemption. We don't add to or complete a perfect work; we enter in and receive it by faith.

Familiarize yourself with the short descriptions below of the steps Christ took to accomplish our redemption. Each piece is essential for you to be equipped to walk a life of fulfillment and victory.

The Good News!

The Bible tells us that the Word became flesh. God became flesh. Jesus was God in a human body. He showed us the invisible God. Not only did he reveal God, but he revealed what true humanity, infused with the Holy Spirit, looks like and can accomplish.

Jesus lived a sinless life. Jesus was perfect. Yes, he had the capacity to sin, but he yielded to grace (God's ability). He chose to submit himself to God. Instead of yielding to the flesh, he yielded to the Spirit, and he did this as man, not God. Jesus accomplished what we could never accomplish. He fully obeyed the law of God.

He was crucified. On the Cross, He became our sin. This is an essential point, which we'll talk more about later. Jesus didn't just die for us; he died as sin. He became sin so that he could break the power of sin over us.

As our sin, he took our punishment. *"The wages of sin is death, but the gift of God is eternal life in Christ Jesus our Lord."* (Romans 6:23 NKJV) He was punished in our place and as our representative. He died the death that we deserved; it should have been us. He was our substitute. He died in our place. Not only did he die physically, but spiritually he experienced the wages of sin, which is spiritual death.

Because of sin, Jesus was separated from God. There are teachings that say that Jesus was not really separated from God. However, sin brings separation from God. It separates the creation from the creator. It disrupts relationship with God on every level. The only way that Jesus Christ could pay the price and restore us back to God was for him to experience every part of our sin and its consequences, one of which was separation from the Father.

Next, Jesus went to hell. This was not to the lake of fire, which is the second death. He went to Hades, or the place of the dead. He became sin, was separated from God, and went to hell. Why? So, we never have to go there!

> **YOUR SIN AND MY SIN HELD THE SON OF GOD IN THE PLACE OF DEATH.**

In hell, our sin held him in death. Your sin and my sin held the Son of God in the place of death. When Jesus was held in hell, when our sins held him there, he believed the Father's promises. He persuaded his heart. He obtained righteousness through his faith, and through his righteousness, he conquered our sin. Not only was he victorious over sin in general, but over our individual sins. If he conquered them, we can be free!

Sin and death could not hold him, and he was raised from the dead. Colossians 2:15 says that he defeated the devil or stripped the devil of his rule and rank. Next, he ascended to the Father and sealed the covenant with his blood as the once-for-all-time sacrifice. He then sat down at the right hand of the Father. It was finished! Lastly, he sent the Holy Spirit to make redemption a reality in the lives of all who believe.

Redemption is complete! The punishment for sin was dealt with once and for all. God is not holding sin against you. He's not holding sin against the world. He's not holding back his promises and his goodness. Through the death, burial, and resurrection, everything we need has been provided.

How do we receive from God?

We receive and access all the promises by faith. The word 'receive' in the New Testament means to actively take and bring to oneself. It is not a passive word.

The scribes, the Pharisees, and the teachers of the law had the Old Testament. They had the Pentateuch. They had the Psalms and the poetry books. They had the prophets, yet they still saw God as angry, harsh, unforgiving, and judgmental. Jesus came and, through his life, ministry, and teaching, revealed a God who was kind, consistent, and easy to please. You probably never thought about God as being easy to please, but Jesus said that all you have to do is believe. He said the only thing that God wants from you is faith. Jesus showed us a God who is approachable and easy to please.

Jesus also revealed that there is no difference between the God of the Old Testament and the God of the New Testament. Religion would make us see God as harsh and Jesus as kind. Jesus brought congruency; he showed us that the God of the Old Testament is the same as the God of the New Testament. The covenant changed, but God never changes!

We need to understand that the Old Testament doesn't give us the clearest picture of God. It gives us snapshots, sometimes cloudy and tainted with man's opinions. When Jesus came on the scene, he said, *"He who has seen me, has seen the Father."* (John 14:9 NKJV) He said, in essence, that if you want to know the character of God, look at me, because everything

I do is exactly the way the Father does it. Jesus shows us the true nature and character of God.

He showed us that the Old Testament laws, rules, and commands weren't put in place to restrict us but to show us what love looks like. Then through the Cross, he gave us grace, the power, and the ability to live to a higher standard than the law ever required. We are free from the law to live a life of love! The way it's done now is through the spirit of grace working through us. Jesus shows the true nature of God. He harmonized the Old Testament and the New Testament God because they are one and the same.

Aligning the lights

I heard this story from Dr. Jim Richards, and I want to share it with you because it illustrates what we are talking about in laying this foundation.

In times past, before there were radio or sonar, when a ship was coming into a dangerous port in the darkness of night, it would keep from being shipwrecked on dangerous rocks or running aground on a sandbar by aligning the lights. These lights or signal fires would be positioned on rocks to provide a clear path through the dangerous waters into the safety of the harbor. By aligning these lights in the ship pilot's line of sight, even in the black of night, the captain could navigate safely into the harbor.

God is full of wisdom. He is so full of compassion that he has given us in scripture the way that we can discover the safe path forward through the storms of life.

Our three guiding lights are given below.

First, the example of Jesus. What did Jesus teach and demonstrate in the Gospels? How did he treat people, deal with sickness, sin, and failure? If Jesus really did reveal God, then anything we read or hear that does not align with Jesus' example of God is either misunderstood, mistranslated, or misread.

Second, what did he accomplish through his finished work on the Cross? Any message, no matter how persuasive, that makes us afraid of God and pushes us to earn what grace has freely given us, is not the foundation you want to build upon.

And lastly, the foundational doctrines described in Hebrews 6, when interpreted through the New Covenant, provide the third guiding light of truth.

When our belief system is aligned with these three foundational truths, it will bring us safely into the harbor. It will empower us to stand firm through life's storms until the promise manifests in our lives. These truths provide the foundation for an accurate and effective belief system.

Chapter Questions

1. How do you understand the term, "The finished work of Christ?" Is your view congruent with what Jesus accomplished in your place?

2. Review the steps that Christ took to pioneer our redemption. How does that compare to what you have believed in the past about the Gospel?

3. Have you subconsciously believed that the God of the Old Testament was different from the God of the New Testament? How did Jesus present God to the world?

Section 2 Faith-Righteousness

Introduction

Dr. Jim Richards

Faith-Righteousness

The issue of righteousness is one of the seven [3]foundational doctrines of New Covenant faith. Jesus, himself, is the cornerstone who brings all the pieces together. The cornerstone holds all the other foundational stones in place. They are interdependent, one upon the other. As the logos, none of them can stand alone. If we change or deny any of the foundational doctrines, they all lose relevance.

Please make a note: Scripture doesn't say that doctrine "about Jesus" is the cornerstone. He is the cornerstone. All Scripture, including these foundational doctrines, only reaches its fullest expression and value as it is expressed through his life. All truth is understood by seeing how it was taught and applied in his life!

It is equally imperative to recognize that Scripture doesn't say Jesus simply makes us righteous. It says he is our righteousness. We do not share in his righteousness as the result of something that is given from him to us. We share in his righteousness because we are in him, and he is in us. It is about sharing his life in every way possible.

These foundational stones not only keep us on track with sound doc-

3   Many believe there are six doctrines that make up the foundational doctrines. After decades of embracing that concept, I felt for many reasons that righteousness should be included in the list of foundational doctrines. And should be considered the seventh of the foundational doctrines.

trine, but when believed in the heart, they shape the absolute truth of the character and nature of God within us! They don't become a substitute for Jesus; they allow us to see and experience him as he is, thereby manifesting the reality of God! What is not seen, experienced, and understood in Jesus is not life; it is merely information about Jesus!

All believers are called to be stewards, i.e., (managers) of the riches of God. The most important resource we are to manage is our heart. This is what the Scripture is referring to when it says, *"Keep and guard your heart with all vigilance and above all that you guard, for out of it flow the springs of life."* (Proverbs 4:23 AMP)

The phrase "springs of life" could be translated as "boundaries of life." Boundaries determine what can get into and flow out of our hearts! They also determine the limits of our lives, whether they keep us in a repetitive cycle of self-destruction or they move us into expanding boundaries that allow our lives to be larger and better. Everything about the quality of our life is a direct overflow of the beliefs of the heart.[4] All God will do in us and through us, whether great or small, will happen because of the beliefs of our hearts.

All beliefs of the heart are governed by two core beliefs: Is God who he says he is, in Jesus, and am I whom he says I am in Jesus? I must believe the truth about God based on what Jesus showed me about him. Likewise, I must believe the truth about what Jesus showed me about mankind. According to Scripture, Jesus was the exact representation of God (Hebrews 1:3), and the Word made flesh (John 1:12). If we want to see God, we must look at Jesus.

Additionally, Jesus did all he did as a man filled with the Holy Spirit. He had authority on the earth because he was the Son of man. (John 5:27) He yielded to the Holy Spirit just as I can (Acts 10:38), and I can do anything He did (John 14:12). Even though he was God, he emptied himself and became as a man, to model the life all men could have. (Philippians 2:5-11)

The two most crucial capacities of the heart are to provide our sense of personal identity and our perceived identity of God. These two dynam-

---

[4] To discover the biblical principles of the heart check Moving Your Invisible Boundaries

ics are the core from which all other beliefs and behaviors emerge. They determine the scope and intensity of the boundaries of our hearts. When we first see God as he proclaimed himself to be, then and only then, can we discover and experience who he has made us to be in the Lord Jesus. Until these two dimensions are in harmony with God, we will never experience the life of God to its fullest expression. But make no mistake; we can only see him as he is and ourselves as we are when seen in Jesus!

One of the fundamental concepts of righteousness is to be "straight." When a path is straight, it is easy to navigate; it is unlikely we will lose our way, and among other things, there are no hidden dangers. One of the more subtle attributes of "straight" is the fact that it is easy to harmonize or align our steps. There must be harmony in the way we see God and the way we see ourselves. If not, it is not a straight path. Additionally, there must be harmony within our spirit, soul, and body. Paul prayed this prayer, *"Now may the God of peace Himself sanctify you completely; and may your whole spirit, soul, and body be preserved blameless at the coming of our Lord Jesus Christ."* (1 Thessalonians 5:23-24 NKJV)

> THERE MUST BE HARMONY IN THE WAY WE SEE GOD AND THE WAY WE SEE OURSELVES.

Sanctification is just like righteousness, salvation, healing, or any other aspect of the life of God. All things are ours because we are in Jesus. They are freely given. Something being freely given doesn't, however, mean it has been received and experienced. We only experience what we receive. The word "receive" means to take hold and bring it unto one's self (by faith). Sanctification, which is ours because we are in Christ, must be something we desire and choose. We must desire to set ourselves apart from one thing in order to align with or enter into something else.

New Covenant sanctification believes Jesus is sanctified. Since we are "in Him," we, too, are sanctified. He has made it a legal and positional reality. But we enter into experiencing this as our reality when we believe and enter into this reconciliation. It is possible only because we are in Jesus, and he is sanctified.

2 Corinthians 5:18-20 is the perfect place to grasp this continuum of what has been given freely and how it must be entered into by choice.

Paul clearly states that we have been reconciled to God through Christ. In verse 20, He says, *"We implore you to be reconciled to God."*

As witnesses and ministers, we are to proclaim the message of reconciliation that has been provided by the Lord Jesus and encourage people to enter into that which God has done. By harmonizing our decisions with God's actions, we experience the life of God.

> **THE ONLY WAY TO HAVE A STRAIGHT HEART IS TO ALIGN OUR BELIEFS WITH GOD'S WORD, HIS NAME, AND JESUS' FINISHED WORK!**

The only way to have a straight (righteous) heart is to align our beliefs with God's Word, his name, and Jesus' finished work! The only way to have a straight soul is to align our thoughts, emotions, and decisions with the same. The only way to have a straight body is to align our desires with the same.

When there is deviation or disharmony, i.e., unrighteousness, in any of these areas, it affects our quality of life. Proverbs 17:20, in the KJV, states, *"He that hath a froward heart findeth no good...."* In Hebrew, the word "froward" is the same as "crooked." One of the most devastating consequences of a crooked heart is that it cannot find good! It will never perceive the goodness of God or the goodness of righteousness in Christ.

The root word for "froward," in Hebrew, is spelled "Ayin-Qof-Shen." The "Ayin" represents spiritual insight and perception. When the heart is twisted (crooked), it perceives God improperly. A misunderstanding of God's identity and character creates a faulty understanding of self.

The "Qof" represents sanctification or the lack thereof. As our heart loses its capacity for understanding and insight, we seldom set ourselves apart from those things that destroy us. If we have a negative perverted view of God, we don't actually desire to set ourselves apart unto him. We twist our doctrines to justify our behavior. Some may tout their legal and positional sanctification in Jesus as a means to minimize the need for personal sanctification by faith.

The "Shin" is about passion and transformation. When our passions are out of harmony with God, they generally align with the lusts of the flesh.

Introduction

We look for fulfillment in all the wrong ways. Instead of experiencing transformation into our true identity, in Christ, we conform to a life that is out of harmony with God but in harmony with the world. (Romans 12.2)

As our heart is hardened and our understanding becomes darkened, we forget that being legally and positionally sanctified does nothing to benefit our lives if we have not sanctified Jesus in our heart. (1 Peter 3:15) In this insidious process, we experience one of the greatest spiritual paradoxes possible. We have the life of God given to us, but we lose our capacity to connect to and experience it.

> *This I say, therefore, and testify in the Lord, that you should no longer walk as the rest of the Gentiles walk, in the futility of their mind, 18 having their understanding darkened, being alienated from the life of God, because of the ignorance that is in them, because of the blindness of their heart; 19 who, being past feeling, have given themselves over to lewdness, to work all uncleanness with greediness.*

(Ephesians 4:17-19 NKJV)

The foundations of the faith equip us to embrace faith-righteousness without twisting it into a destructive license to sin. They keep us on track in the Path of Righteousness, which keeps our hearts clear to see God as he is and ourselves as we are in Jesus.

The apostle Paul speaks of the breastplate of righteousness as part of the armor of God. This is a reference to the ephod worn by the priest in the Old Testament. The breastplate is a vest that covers and guards the heart and other vital organs. There is a wealth of typology in the breastplate, but the main thing we need to see now is how the breastplate and its protection for the heart affect our ability to hear and perceive God more than any other factor.

One of the most unusual aspects of the breastplate employed by the priests was the use of the Urim and Thummim. These two stones were kept in a small pocket in the breastplate, directly over the heart! By using the Urim and Thummim, the priest could pray and ALWAYS get an answer about how to proceed with God. It was the secret key to always being able to receive God's leadership. A heart committed to righteousness is the only absolute assurance we have of accurately hearing and recognizing the voice of the Holy Spirit. When righteousness is our breastplate, it is always possible to stay on track with God.

Faith-righteousness is the stumbling stone of the Gospel. (Romans 9:30-33) This is the issue that causes believers to cling to legalism, swing into liberalism, and become weak in the faith. (Romans 14:1) The inability to grasp faith-righteousness keeps the believer immature and unstable, always searching for some mysterious solution. One of the primary reasons we cannot sort through the doctrine of faith-righteousness is our refusal to build our beliefs on these foundational doctrines provided by the Word of God!

The foundational doctrines give us a "right," i.e., righteous doctrinal base upon which we can build our beliefs and stay in harmony with the Scriptural identity of God. It provides the basis for a heart of faith that will not collapse when the winds blow and the waves crash against it. It will prepare our hearts to grasp righteousness without stumbling at the doctrine of faith-righteousness. We can become mature and stable, blessing ourselves and others.

4. The Power of Faith-Righteousness

The most important investment that we can make in our lives is to walk out this process of establishing our belief system in the finished work of Jesus Christ. The cornerstone that gives direction to our lives and the process of discipleship is both Jesus Christ and his finished work of the Cross.

The Apostle Paul declared in Hebrews 5:12-14 NKJV:

> *For though by this time you ought to be teachers, you need someone to teach you again the first principles of the oracles of God; and you have come to need milk and not solid food. For everyone who partakes only of milk is unskilled in the word of righteousness, for he is a babe.*

According to Paul, a baby in Christ is someone who doesn't know the word of righteousness. This is not talking about a righteousness that we produce in our lives by our right living, but rather the righteousness that is ours as a gift through faith in Jesus Christ.

He goes on to say, *"But solid food belongs to those who are of full age, that is, those who by reason of use have their senses exercised to discern both good and evil."*

The good and evil referred to are not just talking about what is moral and what is not. It talks about truth and error in relation to the Gospel. When we have a foundation and proper understanding of faith-righteousness, we are going to be able to discern whether what we are hearing is accurate according to the Gospel or according to religious traditions. Many contaminate the truth of the Gospel by mixing the New Covenant with parts of the Old Covenant, thus nullifying the power of the Good News. We then wonder why the promises of God are not working in our lives.

Let me provide an example: Many take a New Covenant promise such as, *"By his stripes, you were healed,"* and then attach obedience to a law such as fasting and prayer as the way of fulfillment. When we do that, we are taking away from the promise of the New Covenant. The promise is given for those who believe, not for those who live right, so God will answer their prayers. So don't mix the covenants! Mixture kills the promise. Believe and receive. All things are possible for those who believe.

> **FROM THE BEGINNING TO THE END, EVERYTHING WE READ AND INTERPRET MUST BE INTERPRETED THROUGH THIS FILTER OF FAITH-RIGHTEOUSNESS.**

From the beginning to the end, everything we read and interpret must be interpreted through this filter of faith-righteousness. The one foundational truth that holds every other doctrine of the New Covenant together is faith-righteousness. If you don't understand faith-righteousness, then every other New Testament doctrine will be out of place.

Faith-righteousness is the keystone! The keystone in a stone archway is that one center stone that holds the arch together. Faith-righteousness is the keystone that will hold everything else we believe together. It is the unshakable truth that gives stability to every other area of our belief system. It's what gives us the footing to stand on until the promises of God come to fruition in our lives.

Romans 1:16 NKJV says, *"For I am not ashamed of the gospel of Christ, for it is the power of God to salvation for everyone who believes."*

The word salvation is the Greek word 'soteria.' This word does not just refer to God saving us from our sin so that we can go to heaven someday. Soteria/salvation is all-inclusive for the whole person. It can be translated as healing, peace, deliverance, wholeness, prosperity, and forgiveness. It is the whole package of redemption for the whole person. It is God restoring our spirit, soul, and body to his plan and his design. The Apostle

Paul says that the Gospel is the power of God to produce all of these good promises in the life of the person who believes.

He goes on to say in Romans 1:17 NKJV, *"For in it, the righteousness of God is revealed from faith to faith; as it is written, 'The just shall live by faith.'"* This Gospel reveals the righteousness of God from faith to faith. When you are truly hearing the Gospel, faith-righteousness will be at the center.

The apostle does not say that we go from faith to works, nor from God's ability to our ability, but rather from faith to faith. Faith is putting trust in what God has already provided through his actions for us.

Ultimately, the defining question for which we will be judged is simply put, "What or who is your righteousness?" When we stand before God on judgment day, our list of good things that we have done won't be enough. Our own righteousness will not deliver us; it is only the righteousness of God received through faith. That is the heart of the Gospel. That is the message of the Cross. God makes you righteous, and you didn't have to do anything thing to earn it- just believe!

What is faith-righteousness?

At the forefront of the Reformation of the church that took place in the 1500s was a revelation of faith-righteousness. When Martin Luther stood up and nailed his 95 theses to the church in Gutenberg, Germany, and challenged the whole religious system, what he was ultimately saying was that no one's works are of any value in the sight of God for earning salvation. Salvation is by grace alone, through faith alone. Salvation has to be through the righteousness that God gives through faith. This is the foundation and the very heart of the Gospel.

For most of the last 500 years, however, the church has embraced a doctrine of faith-righteousness that hasn't translated into power that transforms our lives and our sense of self-worth. Why? Because this only can be received by revelation. I would ask you right now, in your own heart, to invite the Holy Spirit to bring revelation of this truth of faith-righteousness. The carnal mind cannot accept it; it is the Spirit that brings understanding.

I want to be really clear that when speaking of faith-righteousness, we are referring to the righteousness that Jesus obtained through his faith. The righteousness that Jesus obtained through his obedience to God, through his sacrificial death on the Cross, and through his going to hell (Hades) in our place. By his faith, he obtained righteousness, and we receive it by believing the Gospel. We experience it when we believe the Good News, thus becoming one with Christ. Any other definition of faith-righteousness is incomplete. Once more: it is the righteousness that Jesus obtained, and he gives it to us when we believe.

Another misconception that many people hold regarding righteousness or justification by faith is that it is limited to a legal transaction by which God declares us not guilty. That is part of it, yes! We were guilty, we stood condemned, and now through the blood of Jesus Christ, we now are declared not guilty. But that understanding has more to do with mercy than grace. Mercy is God not giving us what we deserve. God does show us mercy, and we are not getting what we deserve, but the Gospel reveals much more than mercy; it reveals grace. Faith-righteousness is about grace.

If mercy is that we don't receive the punishment that we deserve, grace is God giving us what Jesus deserved as we are in him! Jesus lived a perfect life. Jesus died in our place. He obtained all the promises of God. He, through his faithfulness and obedience, obtained peace, healing, deliverance, and all the promises. He earned them! He also obtained righteousness, and when we receive it, this gift qualifies us to receive all the blessings. Jesus did what we could never do ourselves.

I love the Thayer's Greek Lexicon definition of righteousness. He defines it as, *"the state or condition of someone who is as they should be."* Faith-righteousness declares you are as you should be in the eyes of God. Most of us think there's something missing in us. We believe there is something wrong with us, but righteousness by faith says, I am as I should be before my Father, and he sees me as faultless. We are in the state and condition of being as we should be before God, and the only thing we did to deserve this is to believe it and receive it.

Here is a great definition by bible teacher EW Kenyan. He said, *"Righteousness is the ability to stand in the presence of the father without the sense of guilt, inferiority, and fear and also the ability to stand in the presence of*

The Power of Faith-Righteousness

sin, death, and the devil as a master." That's what faith-righteousness does in us! It gives us the ability to come right into Father God's presence without any nagging emotions of guilt, shame, fear, or lack. It also makes us a master. It gives boldness to stand as master in the face of trauma, terror, sickness, and death. This happens because we know who we are in Christ Jesus.

Righteousness is the ability of God. It restores our standing with God. This understanding of righteousness is a continuum. What I mean by continuum is that it is part of a whole that, when it's combined together with the other pieces, gives you the full picture of righteousness.

> **RIGHTEOUSNESS IS THE ABILITY OF GOD. IT RESTORES OUR STANDING WITH GOD.**

Let me explain it like this. When talking about righteousness, many churches emphasize the need to live righteously. Of course, that is true and part of the progression of faith-righteousness. Faith-righteousness will cause us to live righteously, but living righteously does not mean we are righteous. When believed from the heart, faith-righteousness will begin to change our self-image. It changes the way you see yourself. If you see yourself as a sinner, guess what? You're going to live your life as a sinner would live. If you see yourself as a sinner saved by grace, guess what? You're going to live your life like a sinner saved by God's grace. You're never going to expect more than just a ticket to heaven. Why? Because you're still a sinner, just saved by God's grace. But if you believe the truth about faith-righteousness, you will begin to see yourself as righteous. You will begin to see yourself in harmony and in right standing with God. Then eventually, you're going to begin to live righteously. You are going to make decisions that a righteous person would make. You are going to have relationships with people in a righteous way. If you're in business, you're going to apply righteousness to your business dealings. Living righteously is not the foundation; it is just the fruit of faith-righteousness. There is a huge difference. We don't live righteously to be righteous. We live righteously because we are righteous. The root is faith-righteousness. The fruit is what faith-righteousness will produce in your life. The truth is the difference between life and death, and discouragement and victory in your relationship with God.

Chapter Questions

1. Define righteousness. What have been some of your misconceptions about righteousness?

2. How does your revelation of righteousness hold your faith together and provide stability in your relationship with God?

3. How could your life be different if you really believed you were righteous apart from your performance?

5. Whose Righteousness?

Many people wrongly assume that Jesus introduced a lower standard of living and behavior than what the Old Covenant required. However, nothing could be further from the truth. In fact, Jesus introduced a much higher standard than the law could ever require. The law dealt, for the most part, with external living and behaviors. People were taught how they needed to live in order to experience the blessings of God in their lives. Now through the New Covenant, everything has changed!

Jesus introduced a standard so much higher that it dealt not only with our actions but with our motives and with the issues of our hearts. Now, because of Christ's finished work, God sends the Spirit of grace into our hearts to empower us to live this incredible life. The game changer is that we are empowered to follow God, not according to our ability, but through grace, the ability of God operating within us.

Jesus said in Matthew 5:17 NKJV, *"Do not think that I came to destroy the law or the prophets. I did not come to destroy the law, but to fulfill it."*

The word 'fulfill' means to bring to a desired end or completion. Jesus didn't just sweep our sins under the rug. He didn't just cancel out the law; he *fulfilled* the law. He brought to completion every part of the law. Everything in the Old Testament points to Jesus Christ and finds its fulfillment and completion in him.

In the second chapter of Colossians, Paul said that the law is only a shadow. The feasts, sacrifices, holy days, and all the commandments are only a shadow. The reality is found in Jesus Christ. You can't have a relationship or intimacy with a shadow. The law cannot give you intimacy with God. It is impossible for obedience to the law to produce relationship. The reality and substance is Jesus. He is the one that fulfills the law and shows us what God's intention was from the very beginning.

In Matthew 5:18-20 NKJV, Jesus went on to say:

> *Surely I say to you that until heaven and earth pass away, not one jot or tittle" (literally not one comma), "will pass away from the law until all is fulfilled. Whoever therefore breaks one of the least of these commands and teaches men to do the same will be least in the Kingdom of heaven.*

You must remember that when Jesus came, he was teaching Jews under the Old Covenant.

In verse 20, Jesus says, *"I say to you, unless your righteousness exceeds the righteousness of the scribes and Pharisees, you will by no means enter the Kingdom of God."* What are you saying, Jesus? He was saying that unless our righteousness goes beyond or exceeds the righteousness of the holiest men of Jesus's day, we won't even enter the Kingdom of God.

We must understand that the only righteousness that qualifies us is the righteousness that's given by God- not the righteousness that we produce by our right living. It's the righteousness of God through faith. There is only one righteousness that will satisfy God, and it is the righteousness of Jesus. Jesus did not come to do away with the law. He came to fulfill it and to bring it to completion.

The purpose of the law was to show us that we can't fulfill the law and that we can't meet the law's impossible standard. The purpose of the law was to point out and tell us that our righteousness is not good enough! The righteousness of God, given through faith in Jesus Christ, is enough. It will qualify us. Jesus fulfilled the law.

Two kinds of righteousness

Ask yourself a question: are you standing on faith-righteousness or works-righteousness? There is really no middle ground. There are only two kinds of righteousness. There is faith-righteousness, and there is works-righteousness. You are either living in one or the other, because if you mix the two, then what you come out with is a form of powerless self-righteousness.

Let's look at a parable that Jesus gave in Luke 18: 9-14 NKJV:

> *He spoke this parable to some who trusted in themselves that they were righteous, and despised others. "Two men went up to the temple to pray, one a Pharisee and the other a tax collector.*
>
> *The Pharisee stood and prayed thus with himself, 'God, I thank You that I am not like other men—extortioners, unjust, adulterers, or even as this tax collector. I fast twice a week; I give tithes of all that I possess.' And the tax collector, standing afar off, would not so much as raise his eyes to heaven, but beat his breast, saying, 'God, be merciful to me a sinner!' I tell you, this man went down to his house justified rather than the other; for everyone who exalts himself will be humbled, and he who humbles himself will be exalted.*

Jesus shared an illustration about two people. The people of Jesus' day would have been very familiar with tax collectors and Pharisees. Pharisees were the most rigid teachers of the Jewish legal system. When it came down to the morality of the law, they were spotless. They lived the perfect life. They fasted weekly. They prayed multiple times a day and tithed from every part of their income, down to the last herb of the garden. Tax collectors were the polar opposite. They had a reputation for being dishonest traitors who stole extorted tax money from their own people on behalf of the Romans. They were cheats, and they were known for being immoral. Jesus proceeded to dismantle the Jewish religious system. The Pharisee, the one who had the outward demonstration of righteousness, was not the one who went home justified, but rather the tax collector who humbled himself and cried out for mercy. The one who looked to God's grace and not his own righteousness was the one who went home righteous.

The person who approaches God with the attitude of "what must I do" will always find one more demand and one more command. Think of the rich young ruler. He came to Jesus, and he said, *"What good thing must I do to obtain the Kingdom?"* Jesus responded in the same manner, asking,

"What does the law say?" (Mark 10:17-22). Every time we approach God with this attitude, there will always be one more thing that we lack. The right response is not "What must I do?" but rather "What has Jesus done for me? How can I receive it?" So instead of looking to ourselves and our works, good or bad, we must turn our focus to Jesus and his perfect finished work.

Chapter Questions

1. How is Christ the end of the law for righteousness? Compare this with Matthew 5:17, where Jesus said that he did not come to destroy the law but fulfill it.

2. Compare and contrast works righteousness vs. faith righteousness.

3. What is the only requirement to receive the gift of righteousness? Do you find it easy or difficult to receive this as a gift? Explain.

6. The Stumbling Stone of the Gospel

Everything you need from God, every promise for healing, provision, peace, and wholeness, has already been provided. Jesus obtained it all through his faithfulness. Faith-righteousness is a gift that qualifies you to receive all the promises in the Bible. It is really that simple. This is the foundation of which you were probably never told.

There is a world of difference between faith-righteousness and works-righteousness. In Romans 9:30-31 NKJV, the Bible says:

> *What shall we say then? That Gentiles, who did not pursue righteousness, have attained to righteousness, even the righteousness of faith; but Israel, pursuing the law of righteousness, has not attained to the law of righteousness. Why? Because they did not seek it by faith, but as it were, by the works of the law. For they stumbled at that stumbling stone.*

There is righteousness by faith, and there is the law for righteousness. Israel pursued God through the law. The believing Gentiles pursued God through faith-righteousness, and they obtained what the Jews were seeking but never obtained because the Jews stumbled at the stumbling stone.

Isaiah 28:16 NKJV says, *"Behold, I lay in Zion, a stumbling stone and a rock of offense and whoever believes in him will not be put to shame."* The rock of offense and stumbling stone that the apostle is talking about here is not just Jesus but this truth of faith-righteousness.

The truth that causes religious-minded people to stumble is not just that Jesus lived, died, and rose again, but that Jesus makes you righteous apart from your own right actions due to putting faith in his faithfulness. This Gospel truth is a stumbling stone to this day. It causes the self-righteous to stumble.

> *Brethren my heart's desire and prayer to God for Israel is that they may be saved. For I bear them witness that they have a zeal for God, but not according to knowledge. For they being ignorant of God's righteousness, and seeking to establish their own righteousness, have not submitted to the righteousness of God. For Christ is the end of the law for righteousness to everyone who believes.* (Romans 10:1-4 NKJV)

Christ is the end or the completion of the law for righteousness! Yes, we can still learn from the law. Yes, I believe the ten commandments are a God-given standard that can benefit society, but the law can never make you righteous. Jesus is the completion of the law for righteousness. God makes us righteous through our placing faith in Jesus. This is the Gospel's rock of offense.

Two examples of faith-righteousness

"Now to him who works, the wages are not counted as grace but as debt. But to him who does not work but believes on Him who justifies the ungodly, his faith is accounted for righteousness." (Romans 4:4-5).

In Romans chapter 4, Paul uses two examples to show us what faith-righteousness looks like. The first is David, and the second is Abraham. Both of these men connected to the righteousness of God by faith. It wasn't complete yet because Jesus Christ had not yet come, yet they had a foretaste of what faith-righteousness would do when a person believes. Both David and Abraham didn't look to their own ability to obey God's standards; they looked to grace. From a natural standpoint, both David and Abraham were anything but righteous.

Think about Abraham. When God called him to leave his country, he waited too long. Then God told him to take only himself and his wife and children. What did he do? He brought his extended family along, also. He made his home for at least ten years in another city before he actually arrived at the Promised Land. When in the Promised Land, a drought came, and God told him not to go down to Egypt, but he went to Egypt anyway. While in Egypt, he tried to sell his wife to another man to protect himself. From a natural standpoint, Abraham was anything but righteous, but God used him as an example of righteousness by faith, because he didn't look to himself. He looked to God and his righteousness. *"For what does the Scripture say? 'Abraham believed God, and it was accounted to him for righteousness.'"* (Romans 4:3).

David is another great example. David was a man after God's own heart, the Bible tells us. At the same time, David had a heart for women, especially a naked woman bathing on a rooftop at dusk. David lusted, he coveted, he slept with a married woman, and then he devised a plan to assassinate her husband so that he could have her for himself. David was anything but righteous in his actions, but what attracted God's attention was his heart. He was looking to God's mercy and grace, apart from his works.

> *Just as David also describes the blessedness of the man to whom God imputes righteousness apart from works: 'Blessed are those whose lawless deeds are forgiven, and whose sins are covered; Blessed is the man to whom the Lord shall not impute sin.'* (Romans 4:6-8 NKJV)

Both Abraham and David show us that we are made righteous by faith, apart from works.

Beliefs of the heart

Allow these statements to reveal what you believe at a heart level about faith-righteousness. Consider:

- You really don't have a revelation of faith-righteousness if you believe that you are saved by God's grace and kept by your performance. You don't understand faith-righteousness if you believe God's grace saves you, but after salvation, it's up to you to perform. It's either grace from first to last, or there's no grace at all. Either God's grace saves us and keeps us, or we're limited to our own ability.

- You don't understand faith-righteousness if you believe that you must do something to qualify for the promises of God. Think about that! If you believe that you must do something to qualify yourself for any promise in Scripture, then you really don't believe in faith-righteousness. Faith-righteousness alone is what qualifies you for any promise.

- You don't believe in faith-righteousness if you believe that your sin can change your standing with God. I know this goes against what is commonly taught in churches. Do not misunderstand me; sinful actions may affect your relationship with God. But the disruption is from our side, not from God's side. God is consistent. He never changes. He never changes the way he sees you or treats you. Sin can corrupt our hearts so that we don't draw near to God, but it can never change our righteous standing with the Father.

- You don't believe in faith-righteousness when you believe you must continually fight the devil. If you're fighting the devil, it reveals that you really don't understand your position with God and Jesus' complete victory over him through the Cross.

- You don't understand faith-righteousness if you are continually looking to someone else as your go-between with God. If you feel the constant need to go to someone else so that they can be that go-between, mediator, or the one who obtains the promise and brings it to you, then you don't understand faith-righteousness. You don't understand what you have in Jesus Christ.

- Lastly, you don't understand faith-righteousness if you believe that you must fast, pray, confess your sin, or do any other action to receive a miracle from God. Of course, there is a place for fasting and prayer, and I believe that we need to be open and honest with God when we make mistakes. But none of these things move God; they move your own heart. They may move you out of a place of doubt and unbelief into a place of being persuaded of the goodness of God, but they do not change God's view of you or his desire to respond when you pray.

- The obvious questions that arise when I teach these concepts include, "Does this mean I can go on and live in sin? Does that mean it doesn't matter how we live?" Paul responded in Romans chapter six with, "Certainly not!" You cannot go on living in sin. It will not affect the way God sees you, and it does not affect your right standing with God, but it will corrupt your heart.

Here are several reasons that we need to live upright and godly lives:

First, when we are living in sin, the sin will destroy our lives. The wages of sin still is death. God won't destroy us. However, the consequences of living outside of God's design will bring destruction and chaos into our lives.

Secondly, if you are living in sin, you're going against your new nature in Christ. In Christ, you have a brand-new nature. When we live in sin, we are living outside of God's design for our lives, and the turmoil is terrible.

Lastly, we don't want to live in a way that gives an opportunity for the enemy to wreak havoc in our lives.

We receive from God not on the basis of our righteousness and ability but because of the standing we have with Christ. Faith-righteousness is the cornerstone of the Gospel and everything we believe. It is the heart of the message. Jesus obtained righteousness, and he gives it to us through grace alone, by faith alone.

Chapter Questions

1. What is the stumbling stone of the Gospel, and why? Where have you stumbled over faith righteousness?

2. According to Paul in Philippians 3, what is the key to knowing Christ and experiencing resurrection power?

3. Have you had the subtle belief that believing that you are righteous by faith will lead you into sin?

4. List some of the benefits that come from believing the truth that you are righteous by faith in your heart.

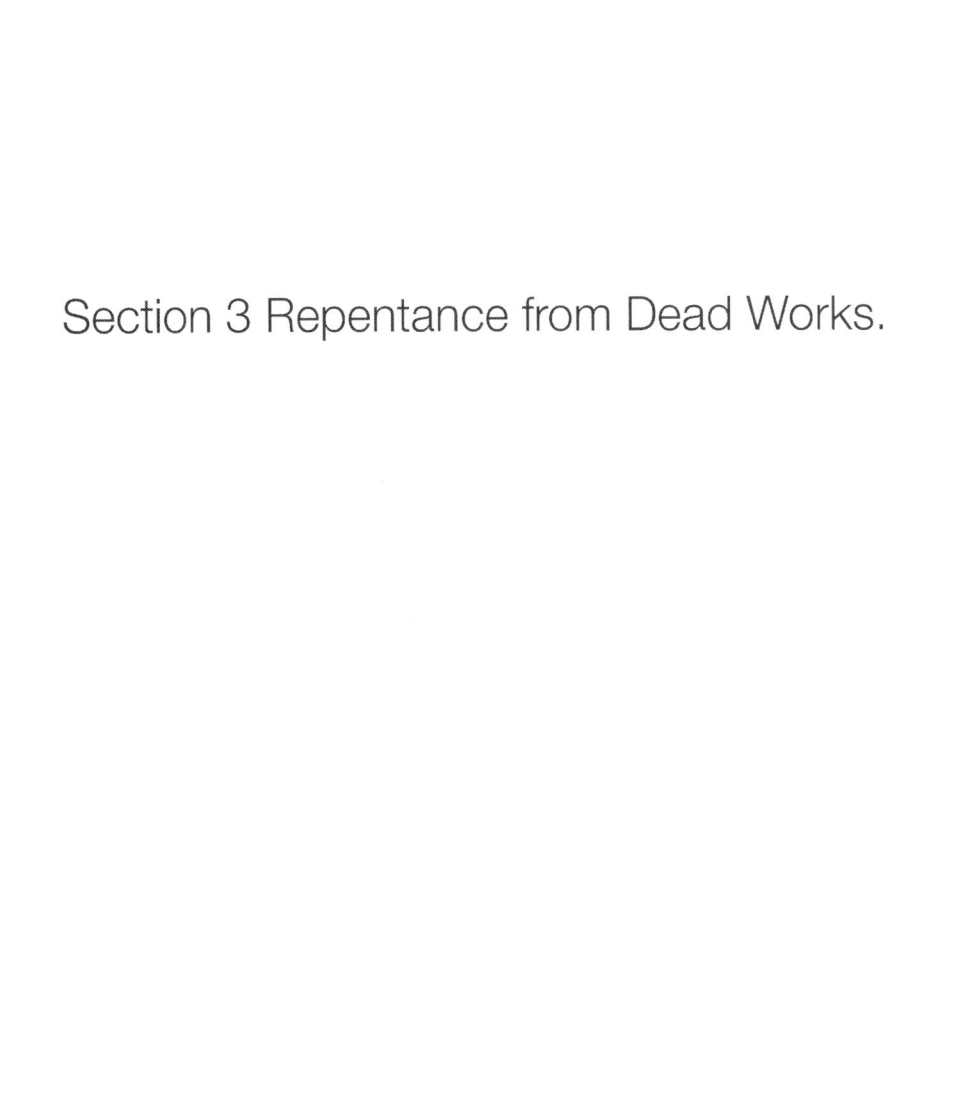

Section 3 Repentance from Dead Works.

Introduction

Dr. Jim Richards

Repentance from Dead Works

There are only two types of righteousness, works righteousness or faith-righteousness, self-righteousness or Christ's righteousness. It is either righteousness determined by our performance or righteousness determined by his! When we rely on our own righteousness, we reject Christ's righteousness. When we accept faith-righteousness, we abandon works righteousness. Faith-righteousness declares, "I trust what you have accomplished." Works righteousness declares, "I trust what I have accomplished!"

Righteousness is a vast concept. Righteousness is the determination of who is right and who is wrong. When we cling to our personal views and opinions, we are exalting our righteousness above God's. In so doing, we are declaring ourselves to be true and God a liar. We are right; he is wrong!

Then there is righteousness which determines our qualifications and approval before God. This is more of a legal and positional righteousness.

All truth is based on righteousness. It is the core for determining ethics, morality, values, fairness, and standards. It provides the logic and understanding for justice. It provides the biblical understanding of love, mercy, faith, and every other doctrine derived from the Word of God. Every biblical doctrine must be in harmony with God's righteousness; otherwise, our doctrine is "crooked," leading people into deception, chaos, and suffering!

Since righteousness is the "Rosetta Stone" for all truth, we can understand why the writer of Hebrews identifies it as the one factor without which we can never become mature and stable. Accepting and agreeing with God's concept of good and evil, right and wrong, brings us into harmony with God, which is another concept of righteousness.

> IF WE ARE RIGHTEOUS, IT SHOULD MANIFEST IN THE WAY WE TREAT OTHERS.

Another interesting concept of righteousness is "as one should be." This can sound a little judgmental or negative at first glance, but it isn't. If one is righteous based on God's definition, he should be kind, fair, and honest. If a person is righteous in relationships, then he or she should be trustworthy. This concept of righteousness is one of the many ways we understand that righteousness is more than legal or positional. If we are righteous, it should manifest in the way we treat others.

Both the Old and New Testaments identify righteousness as the core doctrine with which the human race has always struggled. In the garden, the very first temptation was for man to be a god unto himself. The first indicator of who is god in your world is who defines good and evil. Defining good and evil apart from the Creator is a form of idolatry. It is the basis of everything wrong with the human race. Consequently, we tend to wrestle with this more than any other doctrine. This is why it is called the stumbling stone and the rock of offense. In other words, it is the one truth that causes more people to stumble, find offense, and create division among believers than any other issue.

Since righteousness permeates every aspect of life, faith, doctrine, and interaction with God, it is so vast that it cannot be attained in our own strength or intellect. To interact with a perfect God, we must be perfect, but that is an impossibility. Therefore, God has a dilemma. He created man for the purpose of having a loving family, but sin has made it impossible for a righteous God to be compatible with his creation.

One of the greatest minds in history made this observation. Aristotle rejected the idea of forgiveness "since it involves accepting less than what one deserves." The ancient world understood that righteousness was the basis for justice. If forgiveness is the overlooking or being released from the consequences of sin, it is not righteous. Aristotle's question was this, how can a righteous God forgive unrighteous deeds? To do so would violate God's righteousness.

The current paradigm of mercy, forgiveness, righteousness, and even love seems to be as convoluted as ever. God cannot simply overlook sin. Justice requires that all violations of righteousness pay the appropriate penalty. If God simply overlooks sin, he is showing favoritism. He is ignoring justice for the oppressed. So how does he remedy the problem without violating his righteousness?

He sends Jesus, who becomes our sin, and sufferers all the consequences we deserve. Simultaneously, he lives a perfectly righteous life. He had no sin of his own. After becoming our sin, and suffering the alienation from God that we deserve, he used his faith to conquer sin and be raised up in righteousness.

When we are born again, we are baptized into Christ. We are, in fact, hidden in Christ. We share in his righteousness. We stand in the perfection of his righteousness, blameless before God!

Forgiveness is not God overlooking our sins. Forgiveness is God legally dealing with our sins, in Jesus. Jesus satisfied all the righteous requirements of the law by paying the price. This is what the Bible calls propitiation.

Jesus used his faith to take hold of the promises of God, conquer sin, and obtain righteousness. We use our faith to believe and receive what he has done, to become the righteousness of God through his sacrifice. As Paul says in Romans 1:17 NKJV, *"For in it (the Gospel) the righteousness of God is revealed from faith to faith."* From his faith, our faith-righteousness is obtained, given, and received.

Dead works are the things we do in our efforts to earn righteousness and its benefits. We often think we can earn answered prayers, God's protection, qualification for the promises, and even entrance into heaven by our performance. In so doing, we are rejecting the righteousness of God. Paul said it like this, *"…being ignorant of God's righteousness, and seeking to establish their (our) own righteousness, (and) have not submitted to the righteousness of God."* (Romans 10:3 NKJV)

Dead works, i.e., works righteousness, are the equivalent of trampling the Son of God underfoot, counting the blood of the covenant by which he was sanctified a common thing, and insulting the Spirit of grace. (Hebrews 10:29) It is the ultimate of unbelief and the most extreme declaration of self-righteousness.

All God offers us through Jesus is a promise that can only be received by trusting God (faith). Until we repent of our hope and reliance on our performance, fully giving up the deception that we can obtain something greater than Jesus provided, we will alienate ourselves from God.

The just (righteous) live by faith. (Habakkuk 2:4) As you move forward in the foundational doctrines, be sure to constantly remind yourself that all we receive from God is based on his promises and our trust for what he has done through Jesus. Jesus purchased all we will ever need for life and godliness! There is nothing we could ever do to be good enough to earn these benefits of God, but Jesus freely gives us all that is better than we deserve, which qualifies him to be trusted as our Lord.

7. Defining Repentance

As you begin to understand your identity in Jesus Christ and how everything has changed from the Old Covenant to the New Covenant, you will begin to see real change and stability in your life. Unfortunately, this is not the reality in the lives of most believers. They experience a life that is inconsistent with who they truly are in Christ.

They need something called "consistent theology." What is consistent theology? I want you to engrave this terminology on your mind. Consistent theology is theology that is centered around the life, death, burial, and resurrection of Jesus Christ. Consistent theology happens when the finished work becomes the lens through which we read and interpret all of scripture. If we interpret scripture this way and find something in the Word that doesn't appear to align with Jesus Christ, what he taught, and what he accomplished, then we need to have the maturity to understand that we are not seeing something accurately.

As we discussed in the last section, faith-righteousness is the qualifying factor for us to participate in the promises of God. This truth is also the stumbling stone of the Gospel. Jesus, as a historical figure, is not necessarily that controversial. However, the problem appears when you start believing that Jesus makes you right without you doing one thing right. That's when the message becomes offensive to the religious mind. Why? Because people love their self-righteousness. Self-righteousness makes sense to the carnal-minded.

Like the Jews of Jesus's day, we often prefer to look to ourselves and our ability to be made right with God and then become frustrated because our lives don't match up with the promises that we find in the Bible. Faith-righteousness, when truly understood and believed, becomes an empowerment, not an excuse. Grace is never an excuse to live a life of sin and passivity.

The true message of grace is powerful! It's only when you believe that you are righteous that you will begin to live righteously. What you believe affects how you live, not vice versa. Believing faith-righteousness changes everything.

The doctrine of repentance from dead works

Hebrews 6:1-2 NKJV says:

> *Therefore, leaving the discussion of the elementary principles of Christ, let us go on to perfection, not laying again the foundation of repentance from dead works and of faith toward God, ² of the doctrine of baptisms, of laying on of hands, of resurrection of the dead, and of eternal judgment.*

The first New Covenant doctrine listed is the *"repentance from dead works."* Before we go on, we need to define accurately what repentance really is. If you're like me, your view of repentance was possibly formed from a preacher preaching about hell, judgment, and exposing your sin. A typical scenario would have the preacher list every sin you have ever committed; then, you would begin to feel guilty. Running down to the altar, you would fall on your knees and beg God for forgiveness. Telling God that you are sorry, you would vow to do better next week. The only problem is that next Sunday, you may be up at the front, doing the same exact thing all over again. Why is that? It would be because what we have just described here is not repentance in the full sense of the word.

Repentance, as defined in the original Greek, is the word "metanoia." A direct translation would be *"to think differently after."* Simply put, repentance means to change the way that you think and then learn to think in a new way. The way that you think determines the way in which you live. Therefore, if all you do is to try and clean up your life, live a better life, confess your sin, and attempt to do better without changing your heart beliefs and thought patterns, you're going to slide back into that same rut out of which you just came. Do we need to live godly lives? Absolutely! But if you don't first change your heart and mind, it's not going to change your lifestyle for the long term.

Repentance, when talked about in the Bible, is not merely talking about changing the way you are living. It's talking about learning to think in a new way. If what you think does not align with Christ and what God says about you, then you need to repent; you need to change the way in which you think. Then by the grace of God, you will begin to think a different way. I can guarantee that when you begin to think differently, you will begin to live differently. My definition of repentance is *"a radical change of your thoughts and beliefs that causes you to turn your life and purpose towards God and his ways."*

Jesus, at the beginning of his ministry, made an announcement. He said in Matthew 4:17 NKJV, *"Repent for the Kingdom of heaven is at hand."* What he was saying to the Jews who were awaiting God's Kingdom was that they needed to change the way that they thought about God and about how the Messiah was expected to come because the Kingdom was already there! If they didn't change the way that they thought and learned to think differently, then they were going to miss his coming. That is exactly what happened. They crucified their Messiah. Many of us miss what God is trying to do in our lives because of our unrenewed minds. Repentance means to change the way that you think.

> MANY OF US MISS WHAT GOD IS TRYING TO DO IN OUR LIVES BECAUSE OF OUR UNRENEWED MINDS.

In John 3:3 NKJV, Jesus said, *"Most assuredly, I say to you, unless one is born again, he cannot see the Kingdom of God."* In essence, John 3:3 says, "You must be born again to see the Kingdom of heaven." When you are born-again, you become a child of God, and you become a citizen of the Kingdom of God. The way you access and experience the Kingdom of God is through a process of surrendering your opinion and renewing your mind, which is also known as repentance. Many people are citizens of the Kingdom with access to all of God's promises and benefits, but as a result of their unrenewed minds, they never experience these blessings.

Many Christians are born-again. They are heaven bound, but they are not experiencing the benefits of the Kingdom of God, their inheritance. I define "*The Kingdom God*" as the realm where Christ rules. The Kingdom operates by laws, principles, and values that are usually opposite to how the world operates. In the Kingdom, all provision is available. Healing is available. We have access to God's wisdom and perspective for life, relationships, business, etc. We might be born-again, but unless we embrace a lifestyle of repentance, we will not experience life lived in the realm of the Kingdom of God.

This is because we have not submitted our perspective, our view, and our opinions for his. It is because we have never embraced a lifestyle of repentance.

Jesus said, "*Repent for the Kingdom of heaven is at hand.*" According to Greek scholars, repentance is not just a one-time action but is present and continuous. Jesus was saying, *"Repent and keep on repenting, believe and keep on believing."* Every time we become aware that the way we see things, that our views and opinions are not in harmony with the way God sees things, we must repent. We need to change the way that we think, and then we need to learn how to think God's way!

Chapter Questions

1. Define repentance. How have you viewed repentance in the past? Is it consistent with the truth of the Gospel?

2. Why is repentance essential to experiencing the present reality of the kingdom of God?

8. Motive Changes Everything

One of the first foundational doctrines in faith-righteousness is *"repentance, from dead works."* Repentance means to change and renew your mind and also to exchange your view and opinion for God's view and opinion.

But what is the author referring to when he says that we are to repent from dead works? In the past, I would read this and think that he was talking about changing from a sinful lifestyle. Should we live upright and godly? Absolutely! But in the book of Hebrews, he is not talking about repentance from a sinful lifestyle but about changing our minds regarding religious works and how they affect our relationship with God. Dead works are the religious activities and mindsets that we hold to in an attempt to appease God, earn relationship, or obtain promises and favor.

We all have a list. It might not be a written list, but we have a list written on our minds and hearts of the things that we feel we need to do to be a good Christian. According to the scriptures, these lists are dead works, and we need to repent of them. These works are dead and lifeless, apart from grace and faith. Hebrews 9:14 NKJV says, *"How much more shall the blood of Christ, who through the eternal spirit offered himself without spot to God, cleanse your conscience from dead works to serve the living God."*

The Bible talks about good works and dead works. Ephesians 2:10 NKJV tells us that we have been *"created in Christ Jesus for good works."* Then in Hebrews chapter 6, it says that we are to *"repent of dead works."* Believe it or not, good works and dead works can be the same thing. The major difference is motive. You can go to church with a right heart if you want to learn about God, grow in your faith, and/or fellowship with other believers, and your motive is pure. This is a good work. Or you can go to church because you believe if you don't go to church, God is going to be displeased with you; this is a dead work. You can read your Bible because you want to know God or you want to understand who you are and what you have in Christ. That's a good work! Or you can read your Bible because you believe if you don't read your Bible, God's going to be displeased with you. That is a dead work. You can pray from either perspective. You can pray in order to grow in your knowledge of and relationship with God, or you can pray as an obligation or as an attempt to manipulate God. As an evangelist, I love preaching the Gospel, but evangelistic ministry can be a dead work if it's not done from a heart of gratitude toward God.

> GRACE REVEALED WHAT WAS IN THEIR HEARTS, AND WHEN THE RELIGIOUS RESTRAINTS CAME OFF, THEY DID WHAT ALREADY WAS IN THERE.

God's grace reveals what is in our hearts. Many times, I have seen people begin to grasp the message of grace and faith-righteousness, and suddenly, they are out there living in sin, they have stopped going to church, and they begin to make terrible choices in their lives. Then the grace haters say, "Yep, it's because of grace. This message is causing them to do those things." But you must remember, grace didn't cause them to do those things; it just revealed what was already in their hearts. They were going to do those things whether they believed in grace or not. Grace revealed what was in their hearts, and when the religious restraints came off, they did what already was in there. For someone who has a good heart and who has the desire to know God and to follow him, when grace and faith-righteousness are understood, they are filled with gratitude and love for God.

Whose list are you going to follow?

The Apostle Paul says that we need to repent of dead works. We all have a list. Every religion in the world has a list. Every denomination has a list, the things that we believe we need to do to be right with God. Christians,

Catholics, Hindus, and Muslims, every religion has their list of what they are required to do in order to be in right standing with their God. The Gospel calls us to repent of our lists of dead works and put faith in what Jesus did for us, his finished work.

Dead works lead us away from trusting God. Dead works cause us to trust in our own ability and not God's, which is through grace. Dead works lead us away from experiencing grace. If grace is the ability of God that works from our hearts, then dead works limit us to our own abilities, and when we are limited to our own abilities, we are living in the flesh.

The Jews trusted their religious sacrifices and relied on their laws, but it was all their own self-effort, and it could not set them right with God. When Jesus came, he said his blood was enough; his blood was sufficient. The blood of Christ cleanses our conscience so we can serve God in the Spirit and in the flesh. As we read in Hebrews 9:14 NKJV, *"How much more shall the blood of Christ, who through the eternal spirit offered himself without spot to God, cleanse your conscience from dead works to serve the living God."*

We need to ask ourselves, what and whom are we going to trust? Are we going to trust the blood of goats and bulls, or the blood of Jesus Christ? Today no one in his right mind is going to put faith in the blood of goats and bulls, but even so, we often look to our own ability and our own lists to make us right with God.

The blood of Jesus Christ cleanses our conscience. It cleanses our hearts from dead works. We no longer need to look to ourselves and to our abilities. Are we going to trust our sacrifices or the sacrifice of Jesus? The sacrifice of Jesus is immensely better than any sacrifice we can ever do for God. Our righteousness will never be enough; it can never qualify us to receive from God. Self-righteousness will never qualify us for the promises of God; rather, our qualification is only through the righteousness of Jesus Christ. (2 Corinthians 5:21)

The problem since the beginning

The common denominator in all religions is self. Right from the beginning, Adam and Eve were infatuated with themselves and their abilities.

They took their eyes off God, and they looked to themselves. Because they were focused on self, they were misled by Satan. In Genesis, chapters 2 and 3, when Satan came to Adam and Eve, his temptation came in the form of a question that challenged God's integrity and their identity. The serpent asked them if they wanted to be like God. The amazing thing is that Adam and Eve were already like God; they could not get any more like God. They were created in the likeness and image of God, but because they were focused on self, they didn't see the lies in the temptation. They already had all that they needed. They were already complete, but they were looking to themselves, and because of that, they fell for Satan's temptation. Now, fast forward another chapter to the time after they sinned. The Bible tells us that their first response after they sinned was to hide from the presence of God. The first emotion they experienced was fear- fear of God and fear of his punishment. They proceeded to sew fig leaves together in an attempt to cover their nakedness. This was the world's first religion, the first dead work. Adam and Eve knew they were naked; they knew something was missing. And so, they sewed fig leaves together to cover their nakedness. Self-righteousness will always attempt to use works to cover a person's nakedness instead of coming to God humbly and allowing him to clothe us in His righteousness.

When God went looking for Adam and Eve in the cool of the day, he asked, "Adam, where are you?" I believe he wasn't calling for punishment; he was calling to bring them back. He was seeking reconciliation. God has always been after our hearts. He's always been after reconciliation, but right from the beginning, Adam and Eve tried to sew fig leaves together to cover their nakedness instead of coming to God and trusting him to cover them.

1 Corinthians 1:29 says that no flesh will glory in God's presence. What is flesh? Besides what we are made of, flesh represents the carnal nature that looks to our ability and works instead of the finished work of Jesus Christ. There will always be someone who is better at obeying the rules than you. The Apostle Paul was one of them.

In Philippians 3:3-6 (NKJV) He said:

> *For we are the circumcision, who worship God in the Spirit, rejoice in Christ Jesus, and have no confidence in the flesh, ⁴ though I also might have confidence in the flesh. If anyone else thinks he may have confidence in the flesh, I more so: circumcised the eighth day of the stock of Israel, of the tribe of Benjamin, a Hebrew of the Hebrews; concerning the law, a Pharisee; ⁶ concerning zeal, persecuting the church; concerning the righteousness which is in the law, blameless.*

The apostle was saying that if you are going to look at your list, if you are going to look at your good works, if you are going to put confidence in the flesh, he can do more! There will always be someone better than you. That's why it's either grace or nothing. It's either all God's grace, or we're limited to our own ability.

Chapter Questions

1. What separates good works from dead works?
2. List several Christian disciplines that could be either dead works or good works, based on motive.
3. How do dead works lead us away from God?
4. How do good works bring confidence in our walk with God?

9. The Empowerment of Grace

When talking about repenting from dead works, what we have repented from is not as important as what we are to repent to afterward. We need to repent from religion so that we can serve God through grace. We repent of dead works so that we can live a life of good works that God created for us.

When we are in the flesh, we are limited to our own abilities. We are limited to our own list of actions that we think make us right with God. When in the flesh, we can never please God.

Romans 3:20 NKJV says, *"Therefore, by the deeds of the law, no flesh will be justified in God's sight."* Flesh cannot please God. Flesh is not just the carnal sin nature. We are in the flesh anytime we rely on ourselves and our abilities to be right with God. We are also in the flesh when we rely on our good works and accomplishments to justify ourselves before God. Flesh cannot please God. Likewise, when we are talking about grace, we are not only talking about God's unmerited favor that treats us better than we deserve, but we are also referring to God's ability that works through us.

What is grace?

One of the best definitions for the word grace ("charis" in the Greek) is *"the ability or the capacity of God that comes through unmerited favor and works from the heart."* This definition includes, but is not limited to, the definition of unmerited favor. Grace comes through unmerited favor; it is unearned and undeserved, but what it does is empower us. Grace is empowerment! It makes us able to do and be everything that God says we can do and become. We don't deserve it, but when grace is received in our hearts, grace becomes an empowerment and a capacity that is far beyond our human ability in the flesh.

> **GRACE IS EMPOWERMENT, AND IT COMES TO US UNDESERVED.**

Grace is not an excuse to live a powerless Christian life. Grace is not an excuse to live in sin and embrace compromise. Grace is empowerment, and it comes to us undeserved (2 Corinthians 9:8; Romans 5:17). This definition of grace may be different than what you may have been taught, but it is the scriptural truth.

Paul said that he relied on the grace of God. He said that the ministry he had to the Gentiles was through grace. When Paul, in 2 Corinthians 12, talked about his thorn in the flesh, he was not talking about sickness and disease. If you read those verses in context, he is clearly referring to the persecution that he experienced for the Gospel's sake. The thorn in the flesh was the persecution that he endured in every place he traveled while preaching the Gospel. When God answered him, saying to Paul, *"My grace is sufficient for you,"* God was not saying, "Paul, just receive what you're going through, for my grace is enough." No! God was giving Paul the key to overcoming his trials- the persecutions that he was experiencing. He's saying, "Paul! My ability, my capacity working through you, *my grace* will give you the empowerment and the ability to overcome what you are facing." This was not a call to embrace his suffering but an invitation to connect to the power of grace and overcome adversity.

Grace is unmerited favor. It is undeserved, and it comes through faith in Jesus Christ. That is what it is. What grace does is give us the power and the capacity to be able to live the life that we have always wanted to live.

Ephesians 2:8-10 NKJV says:

> *For by grace you have been saved through faith, and that not of yourselves; it is the gift of God,* [9] *not of works, lest anyone should boast.* [10] *For we are His workmanship, created in Christ Jesus for good works, which God prepared beforehand that we should walk in them.*

We have been saved by grace through faith. Paul next goes on to say, *"For, we are his workmanship created in Christ Jesus to do good works, which God prepared in advance for us to walk in them."* So, we are saved by grace, but it is also about how we live and how we produce good works.

In talking about repentance from dead works, we are talking about changing the way we think in relation to our religious lists. This means changing the motive, changing why you do the things you do, so that you can now live in God's grace and his ability.

Grace abounds unto and reigns through righteousness

Moreover, the law entered that the offense might abound. But where sin abounded, grace abounded much more, so that as sin reigned in death, even so grace might reign through righteousness to eternal life through Jesus Christ our Lord. (Romans 5:20-21 NKJV)

The law entered so that sin might become clear and obvious, being revealed in all areas. What the law does in your life is to cause sin to abound. If you want sin to increase in your life, if you want a revival of sin in your church, then preach law. Contrary to what religion teaches, the law is like pouring gasoline on the fire of sin. The law increases sin, but grace is the empowerment for people to obtain victory over sin. The law entered so that offense might abound, but where sin abounded, grace abounded (superabounded, overflowed, exceedingly beyond measure) all the more.

God won't kill you; however, your sin may. Sin produces death, but grace reigns through righteousness unto eternal life through Christ Jesus. Let's look at that last part. He says grace, or God's ability and empowerment, reigns in your life through believing you are righteous.

Again, righteousness comes through faith in Jesus. Therefore, when you believe the truth about your righteousness, God's grace begins to work in you, bringing you into an eternal quality of life.

In Galatians 3:1-3 NKJV, Paul asked the Galatians:

Oh, foolish Galatians, who has bewitched you that you should not obey the truth before whose eyes Jesus Christ was clearly portrayed as crucified." This only, I want to learn from you. Did you receive the spirit by the works of the law or by the hearing of faith? Are you so foolish? Having begun by the spirit, are you now being made perfect by the flesh?

According to the Apostle Paul, a foolish and bewitched Christian is someone who started off in grace and has gone back into law. It is someone who begins their relationship with God in grace and is now trying to be made complete by their own abilities. According to Paul, that is an unwise and foolish Christian! He says, in essence, "Oh, foolish Galatians, who has put a curse on you?" Unfortunately, that is how most of us try to live out our walk with God. Religion is foolish!

We know we are saved by grace, but we think that now it's up to us to stay right with God through our works. Let me ask you, "How did you get saved, by works or by faith?" Of course, it was by faith, but after you are saved, how do you continue to grow? The answer is the same. You are saved by grace through faith, and you grow by grace through faith.

"As you therefore have received Christ Jesus the Lord, so walk in Him, rooted and built up in Him and established in the faith, as you have been taught, abounding in it with thanksgiving." (Colossians 2:6-7 NKJV).

God does not call us to go from faith to works, or from grace to religion. The way that we grow and mature and the way that we receive God's promises is to continue trusting Christ and what he has accomplished for us through grace.

Chapter Questions

1. What does it mean to be "in the flesh?"

2. What is meant by the phrase "the strength of the law?"

3. Define grace. Is what you previously believed about grace consistent with the Gospel?

4. What does it mean to frustrate the grace of God?

For further reading on grace, read ***Grace the Power to Change.***

Section 4 Faith in God

Introduction

Dr. Jim Richards

Faith in God
Once it has been determined that we will forsake all of our dead religious works as a basis to move God or solicit his favor, we are at a place to walk in faith. Faith is the core of our relationship with God. Faith, simply put, is trust. Faith doesn't move God; it doesn't cause him to respond to us. It is not a power or a force. It is trust! We all know trust is the foundation for all loving relationships!
Hebrews tells us, *"Without faith, it is impossible to please God."* (Hebrews 11:6 NKJV) The word translated as "please," comes from a root that means "to gratify completely".[5] If faith gratifies God completely, there is no need for religious performance to satisfy God or appease him. This is why repentance from dead works must precede faith in God.

Some think approaching God by faith emerged under the New Covenant, but God has always been a "faith God." Faith has always been the one and only prerequisite for a loving, trusting relationship with God as Father. This was the requirement before the Old Covenant was given, under the Old Covenant, and now under the New Covenant. So why is faith so important? From the time of Adam until this very day, no one has been received and justified before God by any means other than faith.

---

5   NT:2100 (Biblesoft's New Exhaustive Strong's Numbers and Concordance with Expanded Greek-Hebrew Dictionary. Copyright © 1994, 2003, 2006, 2010 Biblesoft, Inc. and International Bible Translators, Inc.)

Adam and Eve lived in paradise because they lived by faith, i.e., they trusted and therefore obeyed God's direction and leadership. At a point in time, they surrendered their trust in God. They no longer wanted him to be the One defining good and evil for them. They departed from his righteousness and chose to define righteousness for themselves, i.e., they entered into self-righteousness. The consequence was sin, death, and destruction for them and all who followed.

Adam and Eve lived in a state of righteousness for one reason; they trusted God. Thus, they lived and walked the path of righteousness, wherein was no death. (Proverbs 12:28) Keep in mind, they didn't earn the right to live in paradise. They were born into the garden. It was their natural habitat until their departure from God's righteousness. They lived in paradise because they trusted and followed God. From Adam unto this very day, all who have been made righteous (qualified) did so because they trusted God. Habakkuk 2: clearly states, "...*the just shall live by his faith.*"

THE MODERN CONCEPT OF FAITH IS ACTUALLY BASED ON DEAD WORKS.

Unfortunately, the last 50-60 years of Pentecostal, Charismatic, and Word of Faith influence have complicated, and to a certain degree altered, our biblical understanding of faith. Instead of faith being focused on God personally and relationally, it has become more about being able to get things from God. The modern concept of faith is actually based on dead works. Dead works are those things we do to influence God, move God, earn something from God, or appease Him! When modern Christians think of faith, they probably think more in terms of how to get things from God instead of how to have a relationship with God.

God has gone to great lengths to ensure we know him, know his will, his warnings, and his promises. When a person trusts God, he obeys, not to earn from God or to gain influence over God, but because he trusts that God is good and reliable. All disobedience comes from unbelief (no trust) or rebellion. Unbelief implies God is not honest or trustworthy, while rebellion is an act of disobedient defiance. If we choose anything but trust, there is no basis for a relationship.

Those who live by faith trust what God has said, done, and revealed about himself. In Isaiah 53, when God describes the work of reconciliation accomplished on the Cross of Jesus, he begins by asking the question, "Who has believed our report?" Faith believes God's report of himself!

When people do not believe God's testimony of himself, they create a concept of God that suits their preferences and intentions. This is the basis of religion. Religion has been described as seeking God on man's terms, while faith is seeking God on his terms. In ancient times people cut down trees, melted precious metals, and hewed stones into shapes and images. They called the shapes and images their gods. Then, they imagined attributes which they attributed to their gods and rules with which the worshipper must comply. This idolatry was designed to quench their internal desire to know the true God, but the idolatry facilitated them being able to satisfy their own lusts while worshipping their gods.

Within the ranks of Christianity, we don't create physical idols as much as we create vain imaginations about God. We leisurely reject God's Word and replace it with our own preferences. We don't live by faith, i.e., trust in whom God has revealed himself to be. We create a god in our own likeness and image.

Hebrews 11:6 says that we must believe God is (who he says he is), and we must believe he is the rewarder of those who diligently seek him (by faith). He is not the rewarder of those who perform for him; he is the rewarder of those who believe him to be who he claims to be.

Nothing God desires us to do is for the purpose of earning from him. If we believe he is good and only good, whether we understand or not, we know that he always seeks our good. The foundations of faith provide us with a doctrinal basis upon which we can maintain the Scriptural view of God as we walk the path of faith-righteousness.

10. The Secret to Steadfast Faith

New Covenant faith does not move the hand of God. It is not a work that persuades God to act. Faith, under the New Covenant, first believes that God has already acted. He acted through the life, death, burial, and resurrection of Jesus. So then, under this new and better covenant, we are not trying to get God to do anything. We are not trying to persuade him to act through our spiritual disciplines, such as fasting and prayer. As good as those things may be for our spiritual life, they will not and cannot move God, because he already moved through Jesus.

As believers who have been made righteous through the shed blood of Jesus, we exercise faith as our response. We are to act on what God already did through his redemption. This takes the mystery out of faith. It removes the difficulty and uncertainty and makes all the promises of God open and available to every believer.

God has promised and made available an incredible quality of life to us as believers. Jesus obtained an inheritance for us through his faithfulness. Healing is yours! Prosperity is yours! Blessings are yours! But there is a great battle that you are going to have to fight. The most difficult hurdle you will have to overcome is not faith for the promises but faith to believe what God says about your righteousness. If you can win this battle in your heart, then you will be able to win every battle and receive any promise from God.

My own experience

I'll never forget a time, years ago, when God startled me with the words, *"Son, you don't really understand the Gospel."* I found myself very upset by this statement. You have to understand why I found this so offensive. I was an evangelist. Though young, I had already led thousands to the Lord. In my mind, I thought that I knew the Gospel, and to a degree I did. The truth was that I had a "but" Gospel.

A "but" gospel goes something like this:

- God is good, but... you have to balance his goodness with his wrath.
- God loves you, but... if you're not careful to live a holy life, he will punish you.
- God forgives you, but... don't mess up because your sin will cause him to hide his face from you.
- God heals, but... if he chooses not to, embrace it and learn what he wants to teach you.
- God wants to prosper you, but... he may choose for you to be poor for his glory.

For many people, God is good, but he is not really that good. Unintentionally, we have created a schizophrenic God with a schizophrenic Gospel. It's impossible to trust someone who you don't really believe loves you. This false concept of God has caused many to run from him instead of running to him. So many sincere Christians going to church Sunday after Sunday have never heard the true Gospel.

Eugene Peterson's Message paraphrase says it so beautifully:

> *But how can people call for help if they don't know who to trust? And how can they know who to trust if they haven't heard of the One who can be trusted? And how can they hear if nobody tells them?* (Romans 10:12)

Sadly, not many Christians have heard the true Gospel and, therefore, have a difficult time operating in faith. Of course, you cannot have perfect trust in someone that you don't think really loves you. But God does love us; he is always good, especially when we are not!

Great faith of great Jesus

Allow me to share something from the lives of two people in scripture who were called out by Jesus himself and declared to be people who had a unique, special, and great faith. What was their secret? What did they possess that caused the Son of God himself to marvel? The answer may not be what you expect. One was a man, and one was a woman. One was a Roman, and one was a Greek. One lived in a town called Capernaum on the Sea of Galilee, and the other one came from a town along the Mediterranean called Sidon. As I have combed over these two stories in Matthew, I have found some things that help me to connect the dots.

The Roman centurion in Matthew 8:5-13 came to Jesus requesting him to come and heal his servant, who lay sick at home. As Jesus indicated that he would go and heal the boy, this Roman soldier suddenly blurted out, *"Lord don't bother coming over—just speak a word and my servant will be healed. I am a man who understands the power of a command. I have soldiers under me."* This man's response caused Jesus to marvel and say:

> *'Assuredly, I say to you, I have not found such great faith, not even in Israel!' Then Jesus said to the centurion, 'Go your way; and as you have believed, so let it be done for you.' And his servant was healed that same hour.* (Matthew 8:10-13 NKJV)

The woman, on the other hand, came to Jesus, begging him to heal her demonized daughter. The disciples tried to make her leave, being tired of her insistent pleading. Jesus appeared to be less than compassionate, insinuating that she was a little dog. What was Jesus thinking? This is a cultural statement that our Western minds have trouble grasping. But more than that, he was trying to draw out from her a declaration of faith that still challenges me every time I read it.

> *But He answered and said, 'I was not sent except to the lost sheep of the house of Israel.' Then she came and worshiped him, saying, 'Lord, help me!' But He answered and said, 'It is not good to take the children's bread and throw it to the little dogs.'*
>
> *And she said, 'Yes, Lord, yet even the little dogs eat the crumbs which fall from their masters' table.' Then Jesus answered and said to her, 'O woman, great is your faith! Let it be to you as you desire.' And*

her daughter was healed from that very hour." (Matthew 15:24-28 NKJV)

Jesus was on assignment from his Father. He was to offer hope to the Jewish nation. His disciples would take the Gospel to the world. This woman refused to be silenced. She reached past culture and past every limitation and walked away with her miracle.

So, what is their key? What can we apply in our lives to see miracle results?

Don't limit Jesus

There are several significant parts to these accounts that bear discussion. For one thing, both this man and woman were Gentiles. They were not born under the law. They were not looking to their ability to do right, be right, or pray right. If they were going to receive a miracle, it would be by sheer mercy. They both prayed the prayer, "Lord have mercy."

Jesus told a parable in a similar fashion in Luke 18:9-14, about a tax collector and a Pharisee who went up to the temple to pray. The Pharisee was self-righteous and insisted on telling God all the good things he had done. His ability to keep the law was his basis for coming before God. In contrast, the tax collector looked to God's mercy and forgiveness, knowing rightly that he had nothing to bring before God. Jesus said, *"I tell you this man went down to his house justified rather than the other. For everyone who exalts himself will be humbled and he who humbles himself will be exalted."* (Luke 18:14 NKJV)

The Bible says that God resists the proud and gives grace to the humble. Humility means looking away from our abilities and qualifications and looking toward God's mercy and grace. There is something about God that causes him to draw near to those who know that they have nothing to offer.

Both the Centurion man and the Greek woman also refused to limit God or to place stipulations on God and his Word. For them, the Word was enough. They did not need a sign or prophecy or a blood moon. The centurion declared, *"Lord just say the word and my servant will be healed."*

The woman told Jesus, "*Even a crumb falling from your table is enough for me.*" To her, just a morsel from Jesus, the Bread of Life, the Living Word of God, was enough! Real faith refuses to put God in a box. It takes the shackles off of the Word of God, allowing him to be as good, as big, and as powerful as his Word declares.

Lastly, both looked to Jesus; they did not look to their faith or lack thereof. As far as we can tell, neither one of them even considered whether or not they had or needed faith. They did not have time- their eyes were simply fixed upon Jesus. They had connected to the source and fountain of faith- Jesus himself.

I am convinced that the key to great faith is to cease all pursuits to achieve or earn faith and to, instead, connect to Jesus, who is both the author and finisher of our faith. The greater Jesus is to you, and the more perfect and complete his Word of redemption is in your heart, the greater your faith will become. Great faith is not a wage to be earned. Neither does it come through our sincere efforts to seek it. Great faith is the outcome of setting your sights on a great Jesus.

Friends, to operate in and receive this great faith, it is vitally important that we understand what side of the Cross we are living on. Are you looking forward, or are you looking backward to Christ's finished work? Looking to Jesus will cause you to connect to Jesus, the one who births his faith within us and leads us from victory to victory.

Great faith is really a misnomer. The question that you need to ask yourself is, "Are you connected to a great Jesus?"

Chapter Questions

1. How do you define faith? Is your definition of faith consistent with what Jesus accomplished through his death, burial, and resurrection?
2. What can you do to activate your faith?

11. The Gospel of Peace

Unfortunately, most of what is preached in church each Sunday is not a message of Good News that breeds steadfast faith in God and trust in his character.

Paul shared the secret to developing real faith in God. In Romans 10:15 NKJV, *He said, "How beautiful are the feet of those who preach the Gospel of peace, who bring glad tidings of good things."* He goes on to say in verse 17, *". . . so then faith comes by hearing and hearing by the Word of God."*

So, faith comes when we hear the Gospel of peace. The question we need to ask ourselves is, what is the Gospel of peace?

To answer these questions, we have to go back to the night Jesus was born. In Luke, chapter 2, the angels announced to the shepherds saying, *"Do not be afraid for behold, I bring you good tidings of great joy which will be to all people."* And then they proclaimed this message; *"Glory to God in the highest and on earth peace, goodwill toward men."*

In America, we are taught to believe that peace on earth, good will toward men, is peace between people. However, evidence from scripture proves that there is more to it. The message the angels were proclaiming was that for the first time in thousands of years, there would be peace between God and his creation.

God has always desired a relationship of peace. Even after Adam and Eve sinned, God worked hard to make a way for people to enjoy a relationship. The reason that he brought the law was to make a way for people to experience his promises. All the sacrifices required under the law pointed to a day when sin would not be covered; sin would be erased, forgiven, and removed. This is what the angels were announcing. Heaven was breaking in; a savior was coming, and peace and right relationship with God would be possible again.

A spiritual roller coaster

Most Christians have accepted the concept of an angry God. They think God relates to them based on their performance. They're convinced that God is happy when they're good and displeased when they're bad. Their Christian life is a roller coaster of up-and-down emotions based on how well they have performed. Peace for them becomes about what they have done for God and not about what God has done for them. Our message and our basis for a consistent and hope-filled life is the Gospel of peace. It is also God's method through which faith comes.

We can only experience God's peace to the degree that we believe God already made peace through Jesus Christ. As Romans 5:1 NKJV says, *"Therefore, having been justified by faith, we have peace with God through our Lord Jesus Christ."* Paul says the same thing again in Colossians 1:20 NKJV, *"Having made peace through the blood of his Cross."* God is not angry. He's not ticked off or even in a bad mood. Jesus came to reveal the heart of the Father to his lost creation. He came to show us the way that God really is and how he thinks about us. Jesus came to restore us to a relationship of peace.

A covenant of peace

Isaiah 53 prophesies the suffering of our Savior in our place. Jesus became our substitute. He took the punishment and judgment that we deserve.

> *Surely, He has born our griefs and carried our sorrows, yet we esteemed him stricken, smitten by God, and afflicted. But He was wounded for our transgressions, He was bruised for our iniquities. The chastisement for our peace was upon him, and by his stripes we are healed. All we like sheep have gone astray we have turned everyone, to his own*

way and the Lord has laid on him the iniquity of all. (Isaiah 53:4-6 NKJV)

Less familiar are the words of the next chapter, Isaiah 54. But we have to remember that this prophecy started in Isaiah 52:13 and continues through to Isaiah 55:13. Chapter 54 describes the results of and what the suffering of Jesus would provide:

'For this is like the waters of Noah to me, for as I have sworn that the waters of Noah would no longer cover the earth, so have I sworn that I would not be angry with you nor rebuke you, for the mountains shall depart and the hills be removed, but my kindness shall not depart from you, nor shall my covenant of peace be removed,' says the Lord who has mercy on you. (Isaiah 54:9-10 NKJV)

"For this" describes what Jesus accomplished through his substitutionary death. Christ's death is like the waters of Noah. God swore he would never judge the earth through water again. He gave the promise of a rainbow to assure us that every time we see the rainbow, we will be reminded that God will never judge the earth through water.

In the same way, God gave us a sign that he would never be angry with us and that his covenant of peace would never be removed. That sign is the death, burial, and resurrection of his son, Jesus Christ. We can be assured of this covenant of peace; we can be assured that our sins have been put away once and for all. We can have confidence that God will never be angry with us again.

Paid in full

Most translators would agree that the words that Jesus spoke, "It is finished," could also be translated as "paid in full." The Greek word used in the New Testament was an accounting term and a legal term to describe how, when a debt was fully covered, the note of obligation was canceled or paid in full. As Jesus hung on the Cross and uttered those powerful words, he declared that once and for all, through what he was accomplishing through his death, burial, and resurrection, our sin, debt, and obligation to God and his law would be finished. For the first time in thousands of years, there would be nothing left to separate us from God.

Because of what Jesus accomplished, the way was opened for all people to be saved. Our sin has been paid for, and the debt is removed, but we must receive it.

God, at this time, is judging no one—not an individual or any nation. God is not mad at the world. God made peace with the world through the blood of Jesus Christ, spilled out on the Cross. For God to judge anyone at this time would mean he would have to ignore the blood of Jesus. Any judgment of a nation or individual would be in direct contradiction to what Jesus accomplished on the Cross. Consider this:

> *Now all things are of God, who has reconciled us to himself through Jesus Christ, and has given us the ministry of reconciliation, that is, that God was in Christ reconciling the world to himself, not imputing their trespasses to them, and has committed to us the word of reconciliation. Now then, we are ambassadors for Christ, as though God were pleading through us: we implore you on Christ's behalf, be reconciled to God.* (2 Corinthians 5:18-20 NKJV)

Read it again. God has reconciled the world unto himself. Now you are to be reconciled to God. Do you see? God already paid the price for the sins of all mankind, once and for all of time. It is now up to us as to whether or not we will receive it and enter in by faith. Though the penalty for sin was paid by Jesus, it means nothing to us until we receive this gift of forgiveness through faith. The Second letter to the Corinthians also states that God is not holding our sins against us. The issue is not our sin; the issue is whether or not you have accepted the payment for your sin. In reality, people don't go to hell because of sin. They go to hell because they reject Jesus, the total payment for their sins.

Chapter Questions

1. Why is the new Covenant called the covenant of peace?

2. With whom did God make the "Covenant of Peace," and why does it matter?

3. Explain why fear and faith don't mix.

12. Jesus, Our Substitute

What is the primary message of the Cross? Why did Jesus 'have' to die? The writer of Hebrews declares, *"Without the shedding of blood there is no forgiveness (of sins)."* (Hebrews 9:22). Paul made it clear when he said, *"Christ died for our sins according to the scriptures"* and *"by this Gospel you are saved."* The Bible is clear! God gave his only begotten son to die as our substitute and in our place so that God's judgment can be satisfied and we can 'legally' be restored to God as if sin never existed!

In the society in which we live, and unfortunately in many churches as well, people tend to shy away from the concept of 'sin' and, even more so, from the concept of God having wrath or anger towards sin. Now, let me explain: in the past, as is also true today, many preachers have focused solely on the issue of sin and judgment. Because of this, the Gospel lost its' real power, and whole generations have been turned off to the message of Christ. I also want to clarify that, though God had wrath towards sin, he has always loved people. His anger is aimed at the sin that has wrapped itself around us. Like a cancer, sin has taken over and is destroying God's good creation to the point that God, without the Cross, was unable to deal with sin without destroying the people trapped within it. The great flood of Noah in Genesis 6 is a primary example. God, in his mercy, had to deal with sin in an extreme way so that the surviving remnant of his creation would have a way to live and thrive again in a better world. In grace, he prepared an ark to rescue all who would believe at the time. He did the same thing a few thousand years later through Jesus!

Jesus and the wrath of God

Though the Bible, in both the New and Old Testaments, speaks of God having wrath, it does not describe God as a 'God of wrath.' He is described as a God of Love. John makes it clear in 1 John 4:8 that God is love. It does not say that he is loving or loves people, though he does both. Rather, he is love; love is his true nature. The true definition of love is found in God. God is love! Nonetheless, God is also holy, pure, and righteous. His holy nature requires that he not overlook sin but that sin be punished. God's wrath has been defined as his *'holy response towards sin.'* If this is true, then how can God maintain his righteousness and, at the same time, forgive us? The answer is an Old English word used in scripture called 'propitiation.' Unfortunately, this word means next to nothing to the modern reader. However, for first-century Christians, especially the ones who came out of Judaism, this word had profound meaning. In Paul's presentation of the Gospel in Romans, it is a central theme, as shown below:

> *For all have sinned and fall short of the glory of God, being justified freely by his grace through the redemption that is in Christ Jesus, whom God set forth as a propitiation by his blood, through faith, to demonstrate his righteousness, because in his forbearance God had passed over the sins that were previously committed, to demonstrate at the present time his righteousness, that He might be just and the justifier of the one who has faith in Jesus.* (Romans 3:23-26 NKJV)

Paul is declaring that despite the fact that all of us have sinned and are deserving of God's judgment, God's solution is through propitiation. God sent Jesus as the one who would represent all of humanity. He was to take the full weight of God's wrath towards sin and, by giving his blood, would satisfy God's desire for both justice and mercy. This is perfect propitiation. Then, with judgment complete, God can declare that guilty person who believes upon Jesus as innocent.

I know that is a mouthful, so let's look at it in a more modern translation:

> *For we all have sinned and are in need of the glory of God.* [24] *Yet through his powerful declaration of acquittal, God freely gives away his righteousness. His gift of love and favor now cascades over us, all because Jesus, the Anointed One, has liberated us from the guilt, pun-*

ishment, and power of sin!

²⁵ Jesus' God-given destiny was to be the sacrifice to take away sins, and now He is our mercy seat[c] because of his death on the Cross. We come to him for mercy, for God has made a provision for us to be forgiven by faith in the sacred blood of Jesus. This is the perfect demonstration of God's justice, because until now, He had been so patient, holding back his justice out of his tolerance for us. So, he covered over the sins of those who lived prior to Jesus' sacrifice. ²⁶ And when the season of tolerance came to an end, there was only one possible way for God to give away his righteousness and still be true to both his justice and his mercy—to offer up his own Son. So now, because we stand on the faithfulness of Jesus, God declares us righteous in his eyes! (Romans 3:23-26 TPT)

This translation puts 'propitiation' as 'mercy seat,' taking us back to the Jewish ark of the covenant. The Mercy Seat was the lid covering the ark. Made out of pure gold, it had two angels set over the middle of the box. Here, God, through a sacrifice on the 'day of atonement,' would meet with his people through the means of the blood of animal sacrifices. The mercy seat represented the 'satisfaction' of sin or 'cleansing,' as well as a place of 'meeting.'

For centuries, the Jewish people, according to God's instructions, would go through these ceremonies. They would select a male lamb, required by law to be 'without blemish.' This lamb would then be taken to the priest and presented as an offering to satisfy God's judgment towards that sin.

> **HIS BLOOD WAS SHED FOR ALL PEOPLE AND FOR ALL SIN. IT NOT ONLY COVERS OUR SIN BUT ALSO PERMANENTLY REMOVES BOTH THE POWER AND PENALTY ASSOCIATED WITH IT.**

They would confess their sins over the head of the animal, signifying the transfer of their sins to the sacrifice. The priest would then butcher the animal in front of the people, pouring out the blood as a 'propitiation' to atone for their sin. With their sins covered by the blood, they could now come before God and meet with him. However, this covering was only temporary until the next time they sinned. These things all pointed forward to Jesus and to the great day when he would make his once-and-for-all sacrifice for sins. His blood was shed for all people and for all sin. It not only covers our sin but also permanently removes both the power and penalty associated with it.

The Bible says in 2 Corinthians 5:21 that Jesus 'became our sin.' He was not only the sacrifice for it, but he literally became our sin. As our sin, he took the full weight of the judgment that we deserved. Like a magnet, all of the sin of the whole world came together and was judged once and for all of time. Isaiah 53:6 says, "*God has laid on him the iniquity of us all.*' In the old days, the temple priest would lay his hands upon the sacrifice and confess over it the sins of the worshipper. Upon the Cross, God the Father confessed over his son the sins of all of us. Unlike in the ancient sacrifices, the sins of the world actually came upon Jesus.

Let's look at what Jesus had to say about this:

> *Now is the judgment of this world; now the ruler of this world will be cast out.* [32] *And I, if I am lifted up from the earth, will draw all peoples to Myself.*" [33] *This He said, signifying by what death He would die.* (John 12:31-33 NKJV)

When did Jesus say was the time of judgment for the world? Now! Not in the future. The judgment for sin happened more than 2000 years ago when the spotless Lamb of God hung on the Cross. When was Satan defeated? Two thousand years ago, through the Cross. He went on to say, "*And I, if I am lifted up from the earth, will draw all people to myself.*" In the original Greek manuscripts, the word 'people' is non-existent. The translators added that word to try to bring clarity. Certain translations will have the word 'people' in italics because it is not in the original texts. Jesus did not draw 'all people' to himself. He did, however, draw '*all judgment' to himself* when he hung on the Cross. This interpretation goes along with the context of the above verse, where Jesus says, "*Now is the judgment of this world.*"

The point that you need to see is that your sin and the world's sin were already judged over 2000 years ago when God dealt with sin on the Cross. The hammer of judgment came down hard on sin when Jesus became sin and bore the full punishment. God is not punishing you or anyone else for their sin. There will come a future day of judgment for those refusing to believe on Jesus, but not for you as a believer and not for your sin. Your judgment has already taken place.

Now we can understand how, through Adam, sin came into the world and came to all humanity. Adam represented all humanity, and his act of sin brought the consequence of death to all people. That is why Jesus had to become a human being. Through his death, he represented man to God and took the full punishment for sin. Sin requires judgment, but Jesus took that judgment 2000 years ago. We owed a debt that we could not pay, and he paid a debt that he did not owe. Jesus paid it all!

Faith and the great exchange

On the Cross, the great exchange took place. Jesus, the holy one, became our sin. You and I, in exchange, became righteous with his righteousness. The Bible says that we have now received the reconciliation (Romans 5:11). The word 'reconciliation' also can be translated as exchange. When we believe and receive what Jesus accomplished for us, we participate in this exchange.

The death, burial, and resurrection are our hope for victory. Jesus not only died for you, but he also died as you. Paul said. "I have been crucified with Christ." What God laid upon Jesus, he will never lay upon you.

Here are some things that this exchange includes:

- Jesus was punished… we are forgiven (Isaiah 53:4)
- Jesus was bruised… we are healed (Isaiah 53:5)
- Jesus was made sin… we are made righteous (2 Corinthians 5:21)
- Jesus died our death… we receive his life (Zoe) (Hebrews 2:9)
- Jesus bore our shame… we share his glory (Hebrews 12:2)
- Jesus endured our poverty… we share his abundance (2 Corinthians 8:9)
- Jesus endured rejection… we are accepted (Ephesians 1:5-6)

- Jesus was made a curse... we enter into the blessing (Galatians 3:13)

- Jesus was separated from the Father... we call God "Abba" Father (Matthew 27, Romans 8:15)

- Jesus was forsaken... God will never leave us or forsake us (Matthew 27:46, Hebrews 13:5)

- Jesus bore God's wrath...we live without fear of wrath (Isaiah 53, Romans 5:1, 8-11)

- Jesus was condemned...we are free from condemnation (Romans 8:1)

Galatians 5:6 AMP says, *"For if we are in Christ Jesus, neither circumcision nor uncircumcision counts for anything, but only faith activated and energized and expressed and working through love."* It is the love of God expressed through the Gospel that activates, energizes, and causes our faith to work. The more you meditate on and establish yourself in the truth of the finished work of Christ, the more you will find steadfast faith working in your life.

Chapter Questions

1. Give your definition of the Gospel of Peace.

2. What does reconciliation mean for you?

3. Define propitiation. How does that affect how you approach God?

For further reading, we recommend Dr. Jim Richards' book, <u>The Gospel of Peace</u>.

Section 5. Teachings of Baptisms

Introduction

Dr. Jim Richards

The Doctrine of Baptisms

The doctrine of baptism is crucial if the new believer seeks to live and move in the power of God! A combination of abandoning baptism altogether and failing to use baptism as designed by scripture ensures that a new believer will seldom begin their walk with God in faith!

While there are allusions to the concept of baptism being applied to many areas, there are five specific baptisms explicitly mentioned in the New Testament. All of them are significant milestones in our journey of faith that begins with coming out of the world and is consummated with entering into Kingdom Living!

Reconciliation is the exchange that God provided in Christ. He became our sin, and we can become his righteousness. When we involve ourselves in this process by faith, we experience transformation. There is no other process whereby transformation happens in the New Covenant. The Apostle Paul explained it as to Put Off the old man, renew the mind, and Put On the new man. By following this process, as prescribed in scripture, we can experience victory over any temptation and conquer any sin.

New believers are seldom, if ever, introduced to this biblical process which facilitates all spiritual growth. Consequently, they have no idea how the walk of faith is accomplished. Without this knowledge, they immediately turn to mystical religious ceremonies and all manner of dead works seeking to grow in God!

Water baptism should be the introduction to the process of Put Off-Put On. This should be the model of transformation we follow throughout our entire life of faith. If this were the starting place for all new converts, fewer believers would struggle, and they would completely avoid the lure of legalism and performance-based Christianity!

In water baptism, we participate in a ceremony, which we combine with faith to create a heart belief about our participation in the death, burial, and resurrection of Jesus. Until the death, burial, and resurrection of Jesus becomes a shared experience, it has no influence on our lives.

When plunged into the water, the participant should consciously determine, "I am crucified with Christ. I have died with Him, and sin has no power over me." When we are pulled up out of the water, we should inwardly acknowledge, "I am raised up with Christ in newness of life. I am dead to sin and alive to righteousness."

Romans 8:29 NKJV explains, *"For whom He (God) foreknew, He also predestined to be conformed to the image of His Son, that He might be the firstborn among many brethren."*

Predestination doesn't mean God determined who would make this journey. But it does mean he predetermined how the process would work. He made it a process of faith so the promise would be sure to anyone and everyone. This process is so significant it was determined before the world was created, before man was created, and before the first sin was ever committed. This was a preemptive act of love on God's part!

So, what did God predestine? He predestined that all humans could share in the death, burial, and resurrection of Jesus. The word "conformed" means jointly formed.[6] This is where and how we enter into the resurrected life.

Jesus became our sin on the Cross. In the grave, he suffered the ultimate consequences of our sin. Through the resurrection, he was raised in righ-

---

[6] NT:4832, (Biblesoft's New Exhaustive Strong's Numbers and Concordance with Expanded Greek-Hebrew Dictionary. Copyright © 1994, 2003, 2006, 2010 Biblesoft, Inc. and International Bible Translators, Inc.)

teousness. This is Paul's gospel. (1 Corinthians 15:3-4) This is what a new convert should know and believe to qualify for baptism.

When we believe this Scriptural version of the Gospel, we actually into this experience with Jesus. The Scriptural term for this is "fellowship." Fellowship is not when we break bread together. Fellowship is often translated as communion. In Greek, it is the word "Koinonia." Koinonia is when two share together with something which legally only belongs to only one. Jesus legally fought and won the battle, but by faith, we get to share in it. He is the conqueror, but we are more than conquerors.

When we believe in our hearts what Jesus accomplished, we jointly participate and are conformed just as he is. He died on the Cross. We died with Him. He paid the price for our sins; we were in the grave with him. He used his faith to conquer sin; we were raised up with him. He received the righteousness of God; we receive the righteousness of God with him. He lives eternally by the power of resurrection life. We live eternally by that same power. He received an inheritance from God. We share in that inheritance. He obtained a covenant with God; we become beneficiaries of that same covenant!

> WHEN WE BELIEVE IN OUR HEARTS WHAT JESUS ACCOMPLISHED, WE JOINTLY PARTICIPATE AND ARE CONFORMED JUST AS HE IS.

Although Jesus had become sin, he was transformed into his eternal image and identity. We share that same identity. As he is now, so are we in this world (now). (1 John 4:17) He is the firstborn of many brethren. We are in the exact image of our elder brother.

Whether there is or isn't a ceremony, every phase of our transformation is to die to who we are outside of Christ (put off the old man), renew the mind (consider it so), and be raised up in newness of life (put on the new man). This is the resurrection life to which we are called. This is the process that God foreordained to bring it to pass. Through this process, we have no need for dead religious works or religious processes. We can't do it in our own power; we can only do it through the supernatural power of faith and grace.

No matter which baptism we are considering or what new step of faith we are taking, this is the only way of transformation. Baptism holds the key to understanding the life of transformation by faith.

13. The Significance of Baptism

Everything we believe about ourselves, God, and the Gospel must be filtered through the sterling truth of what Jesus revealed about God, what Jesus accomplished through his death, burial, and resurrection, and lastly, the foundations of the New Covenant, as described in Hebrews chapter six.

The teaching of baptism is no different. We need to approach this important doctrine through the lens of faith-righteousness, grace, and the finished work of the Cross.

Hebrews 6:2 says, "the doctrine of baptisms." It does not say baptism, singular, but baptisms, plural. It's not a single baptism; there are multiple baptisms described in scripture. In these next three chapters, we are going to talk about three baptisms that are very clearly taught in scripture and are part of the New Covenant.

Baptisms in scripture

Under the Old Covenant, there were different ceremonial washings or baptisms. Even when we read the Gospels, you have John the Baptist performing the baptism of repentance. Please remember that the New Covenant started when Jesus Christ rose from the dead. Jesus cut the covenant and inaugurated it in his own blood. Even in the Gospels, Jesus was operating under the Old Covenant. I am not saying that what Jesus taught wasn't true or that we can't apply it to our lives, but that Jesus was fulfilling the Old Covenant and ushering us into the time we currently live in. Jesus was a teacher of the Kingdom. He was showing us through his life and teaching how we would operate in the Kingdom of God through the New Covenant that he was bringing. The New Covenant was established by Jesus Christ's resurrection. There were different baptisms under the Old Covenant, and we can learn from them, but they all point forward and find their fulfillment in what Jesus accomplished through his death, burial, and resurrection.

I want to touch on one example of baptism under the Old Covenant that was a type and shadow of New Covenant baptism. It took place when God took the children of Israel out of bondage in Egypt. He did this by the blood of the lamb. On the night that they left Egypt, God told them to sacrifice a lamb and put the blood of the lamb over the lintel of the door. The blood represented deliverance from wrath through a blood sacrifice. God then led them out of Egypt, which was a type of the world. Jesus leading them out was a type of the New Birth, out of bondage and out of slavery to sin. He led them up to the banks of the Red Sea, and as the armies of Egypt were coming down upon the children of Israel, God then opened the Red Sea before them, and they went through the sea on dry ground. The children of Israel crossed through the Red Sea, through those waters of baptism. The enemy was cut off and destroyed. His hold was cut off from their lives, and they came out on the other side completely free.

> **EVERYTHING THAT TOOK PLACE UNDER THE OLD COVENANT WAS A SHADOW OF WHAT WOULD FIND FULFILLMENT IN JESUS CHRIST. JESUS IS THE FULFILLMENT.**

Apostle Paul, in 1 Corinthians 10, relates this to baptism. Everything that took place under the Old Covenant was a shadow of what would find fulfillment in Jesus Christ. Jesus is the fulfillment. We can draw wisdom from these types and shadows. You cannot have a relationship with the shadow, but it will point you to the reality. There is always a substance beyond the shadow, and Jesus is that substance behind the types and shadows in the Old Covenant.

What is baptism?

Baptism is powerful. When we talk about baptism scripturally, we are referring to taking one thing and immersing it into another thing until only one thing remains. The Greek word for baptism was actually a word that they used in bible times for dying linen cloth. They would take a clean white cloth and would immerse it into a color until there was no separating the cloth from the dye. The two had become one. When we are talking about baptism, we are talking about becoming one in this immersion process that takes place. In historical literature, it is also used to describe a ship sinking at sea and being completely immersed under the waters.

The picture we have of baptism is that of being completely immersed in something else until you become one with it. However, baptism, like any ceremony, if not combined with grace and faith, is only a lifeless doctrine. It's when there is a faith connection that it becomes a powerful demonstration of what took place and is taking place in your life.

I'll never forget an experience that I had when I was in a certain Muslim nation. In that nation, there is widespread persecution against Christians. As it started out, I was driven to a compound on the outside of town, and as we pulled up to the gates, there were armed men at the gates. They brought me to a courtyard where there was a little pool of water and where ten converts from Islam had come out to be baptized. They heard that there was a foreign missionary in town, and they wanted to be baptized. Please understand that in many churches, baptism is just a ceremony and a tradition. In the Muslim culture, one can pray a prayer for salvation, and that can be forgiven. But if you go down into the waters of baptism into Christ, Islam believes that it is the point of no return. If you're baptized in water, you have cut off all ties to your religion, the Islamic god, and your family.

As I stood there with these Muslim brothers and sisters that had come out of Islam, being born- again into Christ, I saw the significance firsthand of what it really means to be baptized in water. They were identifying themselves with Jesus Christ, going down into death with him, leaving their old life, identity, and family. They were declaring their oneness with Christ and being raised up into new life. Baptism, combined with faith, is incredibly powerful. What an experience!

Several years ago, my Brazilian-born wife became a US citizen. She had been living in America for many years, but when the citizenship ceremony took place, and she swore allegiance to the United States of America, that ceremony transitioned her into a new place and position. I think that this is very similar to baptism. It is a ceremony that transfers you into a whole new set of rights and privileges. It gives you a new awareness of what you have in Christ and what you have in the Kingdom of God.

Into the body of Christ

> THINK OF BAPTISM AS A TRANSITION FROM ONE LOCATION TO ANOTHER PLACE.

Think of baptism as a transition from one location to another place. When the children of Israel went through the Red Sea, they were transitioning out of bondage and slavery into the new reality of being free-born children of God. When the children of Israel, after 40 years of wandering in the desert, went over the Jordan and into the promised land, again, they were transitioning from the wilderness reality into that of living in the land of promise.

We need to think of baptism as a transition. The first transition or baptism that we're going to talk about here is being baptized by the Spirit into the body of Christ. 1 Corinthians 12:13 NKJV says, *"By one spirit, we were all baptized in to one body."*

What is the apostle Paul talking about? He is not talking about baptism in water. He is talking about the immersion or the baptism that took place when we believed the Gospel. When we believed upon Jesus Christ as our Lord and Savior, we were baptized by the Spirit into Christ's body. When you were born-again, you put on Christ.

To learn more about the new you, "in Christ," read through the book of Ephesians and underline every time it says, "in Christ." We have become united or identified with Christ through the death, burial, and resurrection of Jesus and through putting faith in what he accomplished.

When we are baptized into the body of Christ, the first baptism, we become part of a new family because we are in Christ. God is our Father, and we are his children. Jesus Christ is our older brother. We are also part of a new Kingdom. The Kingdom is the rule and the reign of God; it is that realm where Christ is king. As I said before, when you are born-again, you have the capacity to see and experience the benefits of the Kingdom of God. But most people will live their whole Christian life and never experience the benefits of the Kingdom. Why? Because they never embrace the process of repentance or changing their thoughts and beliefs through the renewing of their minds.

We also have a new citizenship as a result of being baptized into the body of Christ. Our citizenship is the Kingdom of God. Just like in the case of my wife, where she became a citizen of the United States, she now has new access, rights, and privileges. These were things that she didn't have before. In the same way, we have rights and privileges that we did not have before we met Christ. All the rules of life changed when you became a citizen of the Kingdom of God. So now, you, as a child of God, baptized into the body of Christ, have rights and privileges. You are a citizen and part of the Kingdom. This is the Good News.

Chapter Questions

1. What is needed to turn a ceremony into a life-giving experience?
2. What are the three main baptisms discussed in the New Covenant?
3. What does it mean to be baptized into the body of Christ?
4. How is baptism a way to experience the "Sozo of God?

14. Water Baptism

The second life transition or baptism is the baptism in water. When you go through the book of Acts, you will notice that whenever the Gospel was preached, the people who believed were baptized in water. A perfect example is seen in Acts 8:26-40. When God sent Philip the Evangelist out into the desert, he had prepared an Ethiopian to hear the Gospel. It says that as Philip came along, he heard this Ethiopian man reading from the book of Isaiah. Philip came up with him in the chariot and began to share the Gospel. As they rode along, they saw some water, and the Ethiopian man said, "*What is to keep me from being baptized?*"

Notice Philip's response. He says, "*If you believe that Jesus Christ is the son of God, you may be baptized,*" and then the Ethiopian replies, "*I believe that Jesus Christ is the son of God.*" They stopped the chariot, and Philip and the eunuch went down into the water for baptism.

The interesting thing in the story is that this Ethiopian was a brand-new Christian; he had only been born-again for a matter of minutes, and Philip was willing to baptize him. This tells us that the early church believed that we should be quick to baptize new believers. Nowhere in the book of Acts do you see someone coming to Christ and then being told to come to a multi-day class and, at the end of that class, finally being baptized. No! It was immediate. It proceeded directly after their confession of faith in Jesus Christ.

Please note, when you read through the book of Acts, you will notice that any believer could do the baptizing. Who does the baptizing is not as important as the candidate's confession of faith and what is happening in their hearts. The only prerequisite for baptism is to believe the Gospel.

Experiencing the benefits

Mark 16:16 NKJV, *"He who believes and is baptized will be saved; but he who does not believe will be condemned."* This is the scripture that different denominations use to emphasize that to be saved, you must be baptized. But that is not what the scripture as a whole teaches. Salvation is by grace, through faith. It's by you putting faith in what Jesus Christ did on the Cross. The only prerequisite to being saved is to believe the Gospel.

> SOZO IS AN ALL-INCLUSIVE WORD THAT COVERS EVERYTHING THAT JESUS CHRIST PROVIDED THROUGH HIS DEATH, BURIAL, AND RESURRECTION.

If that is true, then what is Jesus saying in Mark 16:16? It says, *"He who believes and is baptized will be saved."* As I mentioned before, the word saved does not only mean to be forgiven and to go to Heaven someday. The word "saved" is the Greek word "sozo," which includes "to be saved, forgiven, healed, delivered, given peace, prosperity, and wholeness." Sozo is an all-inclusive word that covers everything that Jesus Christ provided through his death, burial, and resurrection. What I believe Jesus is teaching here is that he who believes and is baptized, making the transition/immersion into Christ, will experience sozo, the forgiveness, healing, delivering, and saving power of God. Baptism is key for us to experience the fullness of salvation in every area of our lives. The key to being baptized and to making that transition into sozo life is to believe. If salvation is by faith, then condemnation and eternal judgment are the results of unbelief in Jesus Christ and his finished work.

You may wonder, "Should I be rebaptized if I did not understand the truth about water baptism?" I am asked this question often when I teach on this subject. If you were born-again but did not understand the significance of what you were doing, the decision to get rebaptized or not is between you and God. I usually encourage people to evaluate their situation as follows: if you were baptized as a child or maybe came out of a denominational background where child baptism was normal or tradition but didn't grasp the significance of what was taking place, then consider being rebaptized, putting your faith in Jesus. Baptism is all about faith. It's all about putting faith in what Jesus did, and if you didn't do that as a child, then be baptized as an adult, putting your faith in Jesus.

I don't believe that you have to be baptized multiple times. If you knew what you were doing, then don't come under the weight of condemnation that causes you to become so introspective that you believe there's something missing in your life. That is what the devil does. He makes us so focused on ourselves, believing that there is something missing or lacking in us or that we're not open and available for God to use us. Don't let the enemy use condemnation on you. Yet at the same time, if you feel the Spirit leading you to be rebaptized, then go for it.

Faith and baptism

Baptism is a powerful demonstration of faith in Christ. Colossians 2:12 NKJV says, *"You were also… buried with him in baptism, in which you were also raised with him through faith in the working of God who raised him from the dead."* Paul likens baptism to being buried with Christ, going under the waters, becoming one in Jesus's death, and then through faith, participating in his resurrection. Baptism is about our identification in the death, burial, and resurrection of Jesus Christ.

Romans 6:1-6 NKJV says:

> *What shall we say? Shall we continue in sin that grace may abound? Certainly not. How shall we, who died to sin live any longer in it? Or do you not know that as many of us as were baptized into Christ were baptized into his death.*

Again, we see the connection between baptism and participating in the death of Jesus.

"Therefore, we were buried with him through baptism into death that just as Christ was raised from the dead, by the glory of the father, even so we should walk in newness of life."

The goal of baptism is to bring you to a place where you walk in newness of life! Living in the abundant life, the quality of life that God provided for you. Baptism is a step in that direction where you identify yourself in his death, burial, and resurrection unto newness of life.

Baptism and surrender

Water baptism is a place of giving up who we are so that we can become the person God desires us to be. It is a place where we surrender every excuse. We've all had excuses. We all have our lists. Baptism is that place where we surrender our excuses and say, "I am following you, Jesus."

If for no other reason, be baptized for the sake of obedience to Jesus Christ. The apostles baptized everywhere they went, preaching the Gospel. People were baptized in water as a sign of obedience.

Lastly, I have seen that when a person is willing to follow Christ into the waters of baptism, it places them in a position to receive the mighty power of God upon their lives. I have watched people that I have baptized experience remarkable transformation. When they would come up out of the water, the Holy Spirit would come upon them with such power that addictions, lies, and bondages were broken.

Remember that when Jesus went to John to be baptized and went down under the waters of the Jordan River, he came up out of the water, and the Holy Spirit came upon him in the form of a dove. It was at that place that Jesus began his personal ministry. Among other things, baptism in water places us in a position to receive the baptism of the Holy Spirit. That is the third baptism that we see in the New Testament.

Chapter Questions

1. What does water baptism mean to you? When you were baptized, were you identifying with Christ's death, burial, and resurrection, or just going through a religious ceremony?

2. What is the significance of baptism into water? Look up some New Testament scriptures that describe baptism.

15. Baptism into the Holy Spirit

The third baptism is a baptism by Jesus into the Holy Spirit. This is often called the baptism of the Holy Spirit. When we talk about the baptism of the Holy Spirit, it can become really controversial. Some denominations believe that you receive it all at the moment of salvation. Others, like those in the Pentecostal denominations, may teach that it is a separate, distinct experience, apart from salvation. I believe that it is, but that it can be both! Allow me to explain. I believe that when you're born-again, you receive the Holy Spirit. The Spirit comes to live in you. You are made a new creation; the Spirit of God dwells in you. I also believe from scripture that there is an experience where the Holy Spirit comes upon you for ministry. This is for the purpose of ministering to people and winning our world for Christ.

To recap, when you are born-again, your spirit becomes one with his Spirit; the Spirit of God lives in you. The Bible also talks about the Spirit being "upon you." In John chapter 14:12-18 NKJV, Jesus said, *"Most assuredly, I say to you, he who believes in me, the works that I do, he will do also; and greater works than these he will do because I go to my father."* We all want to do greater works. We want to do those things that Jesus promised. Jesus tells us how we are going to do them and that we will be able to do these things because he was going to his Father.

What is significant about this is that when Jesus went to the Father, not only had he completed the work of redemption, not only had he died for sin, risen from the dead, presented his blood, and sat down at the right hand of the Father, but that he did even more. The book of Acts says that

Jesus received the Holy Spirit from the Father and poured out what we see on the day of Pentecost.

> *This Jesus God has raised up, of which we are all witnesses. Therefore, being exalted to the right hand of God, and having received from the Father the promise of the Holy Spirit, he poured out this which you now see and hear.* (Acts 2:32-33 NKJV)

Greater works

Jesus is telling us that greater works are going to happen because you are going to receive what he had, and therefore, you are going to be able to do what Jesus did. (John 14:12-14 NKJV) Jesus was a man full of the Holy Spirit. When he came to planet Earth, he laid aside his deity and took upon himself human flesh and blood. Everything that Jesus did on earth was done as a result of allowing the Holy Spirit to live and move through him. Because we have been born-again and made righteous by the blood of Jesus, that same Holy Spirit can not only live within us but can also come upon us for powerful ministry.

> EVERYTHING THAT JESUS DID ON EARTH WAS DONE AS A RESULT OF ALLOWING THE HOLY SPIRIT TO LIVE AND MOVE THROUGH HIM.

There is a world of difference between the Holy Spirit's activity in the Old Testament and the Holy Spirit's activity in the New Testament. Under the Old Covenant, the Spirit would come upon someone so they could perform an act of power or a miracle. After that, the Holy Spirit would leave. Under the New Covenant, the Spirit remains with us. He remained in Jesus, and he remains in us. He doesn't float away. He doesn't leave. We cannot sin him away. Yes, we can grieve the Holy Spirit where we are no longer sensitive to his work in our lives, but unlike David, we don't need to sing, *"Take not your Holy Spirit from me."*

Jesus said that because he was going to the Father, we would be able to do greater works. In verse 16 of John 14 NKJV, he says, *And I will pray to the father, and he will give you another helper that he may abide with you forever."*

Another helper? He is another of the same kind. He is part of the Trinity. And he is called the helper. The Holy Spirit is called the helper, not the tormentor. He's the "parakletos". He's the one who is called alongside to help us. He is our counselor. He's not there to condemn us and point out our faults. Our own hearts will do that, but it's not the Holy Spirit. What the Holy Spirit does is point us to Jesus and make us aware of who we are in Christ. He convinces us of our righteousness.

> *I will pray to the father, and he will give you another helper that he may abide with you forever. The spirit of truth, whom the world cannot receive because it neither sees him nor knows him; but you know him for, he dwells with you and will be in you, I will not leave you orphans; I will come to you. (John 14:15-18 NKJV)*

In John chapter 16:7 NKJV, Jesus goes on to say, *"Nevertheless I tell you the truth. It is to your advantage that I go away; for if I do not go away, the helper will not come to you; but if I depart, I will send him to you."*

Jesus says it is better and to our advantage to have the Holy Spirit than it is to have Jesus in the flesh. That's amazing! The Holy Spirit is here to stay, but he also wants to operate through us. He wants to come upon us with power. In the book of Acts, there is a transition taking place from the old to the new. Jesus came under the Old Covenant. He taught about the Kingdom of God and the benefits of the Kingdom. He told us of the New Covenant that was coming. The coming of the Holy Spirit is what marked the beginning of the New Covenant.

Acts 1:5 NKJV says, *"For John, truly baptized with water, but you shall be baptized with the Holy Spirit, not many days from now."*

In possibly as little as seven days later, this took place.

> *When the Day of Pentecost had fully come, they were all with one accord in one place. ² And suddenly there came a sound from heaven, as of a rushing mighty wind, and it filled the whole house where they were sitting. ³ Then there appeared to them divided tongues, as of fire, and one sat upon each of them. ⁴ And they were all filled with the Holy Spirit and began to speak with other tongues, as the Spirit gave them utterance. (Acts 2:1-4 NKJV)*

This is the first place where the Holy Spirit was poured out after the resurrection, and believers received the Holy Spirit. There are also three other examples in the book of Acts where we have a clear picture of what took place when the Holy Spirit came upon a person. Three out of those four times, it specifically says that when they were filled with the Holy Spirit, they began to speak in other tongues.

This is for you

> THE SAME HOLY SPIRIT AND THE SAME MANIFESTATION THAT TOOK PLACE IN THE BOOK OF ACTS IS WHAT GOD HAS FOR YOU TODAY.

This is the way that the Spirit worked in the book of Acts, and he is the same today. He does not do things one way in the Bible and another way now. The same Holy Spirit and the same manifestation that took place in the book of Acts is what God has for you today.

If you have an upbringing, tradition, or denominational background that taught against these things, it may be difficult for you to receive the gift of tongues. But understand that it is for everyone. It says that they were *"all filled with the Holy Spirit,"* and as a result, they began speaking in tongues.

In Acts chapter 10, the Holy Spirit came upon them, and they began to speak in other tongues, and then they were baptized. So, there is no specific order in which these things need to happen. Acts chapter 8 is the only place that does not specifically say that they spoke in tongues, but it implies that something notable took place when hands were laid upon them. Lastly, in Acts chapter 19, they were filled with the Holy Spirit when Paul placed his hands on them, and they, too, began to speak in tongues and to prophesy. Therefore, what we see and what we should expect is that when we receive this baptism and immersion into the Holy Spirit, it should be accompanied by speaking in tongues.

Don't beat yourself up and condemn yourself if you don't speak in tongues, but rather know this: it is available for you, and you can access it at any time. In fact, the gift of tongues is already on the inside of you.

If you have the Holy Spirit through the New Birth in Jesus, you have tongues and all the gifts of the Spirit. You must come to that place where you desire it. Paul said, *"Eagerly desire, spiritual gifts."* You can go to God and receive this gift because Jesus said, *"Everyone who asks, receives."*

Lastly, to receive the baptism of the Holy Spirit, you can't receive it passively. In Acts chapter 8, Philip went to Samaria and preached the Gospel. Signs and wonders took place, people were baptized, and in verse 14, it says:

> *When the apostles who were at Jerusalem heard that Samaria had received the word of God, they sent Peter and John to them who, when they had come down, prayed for them that they might receive the Holy Spirit. For as of yet, he had fallen on none of them. They had only been baptized in the name of Jesus.*

They then laid hands on them, and they received the Holy Spirit.

Twice in these verses, the word received is used. It says that the Samaritans had *"received the word."* This is a passive tense of the word, as if you're receiving a gift that is being given to you. In the second instance, it says that the apostles laid hands on them and that they *"received the Holy Spirit."* This is a completely different Greek word, and it means that they actively took hold of a gift and brought it to themselves. I believe that what scripture is teaching us is that receiving the baptism of the Holy Spirit is not done passively. You are not only receiving something that's been freely given, but you're laying hold of it, and you are bringing it to yourself. That is the way we receive not only the gift of the Holy Spirit but every promise of God. They must be actively, not passively, received.

Let me recap the three New Covenant baptisms discussed here. The first is by the Spirit into the body of Christ, and that takes place at salvation. The second is baptism by another believer into water, where we identify ourselves with the death, burial, and resurrection of Jesus. The third is the baptism by Jesus into the Holy Spirit and power.

Chapter Questions

1. What is the baptism in the Holy Spirit?

2. How did the Spirit's activity with man differ from the Old Covenant to the New?

3. Write out several benefits of speaking in tongues. Are you making use of this gift in your personal life with God?

4. Explain the difference between passively and actively receiving from God.

5. Have you received the baptism of the Holy Spirit, as the disciples did in the book of Acts? If not, take a few minutes to ask the Father and receive this gift.

Section 6 Laying On Of Hands

Introduction

Dr. Jim Richards

Laying On of Hands

Laying on of hands presents some very interesting concepts that start with personal development, to personal ministry, and reach into the ultimate expression of reconciliation.

The most pronounced example of laying on of hands occurs when the priest would lay hands on a sin offering to transfer the sin of the worshipper to the animal to be sacrificed. This is a type of what God did in Isaiah 53:6, where God laid our sin on Jesus.

The sacrificial animal would die the death the worshipper deserved to die, just as Jesus, after becoming our sin, died the death we deserve to die. He becomes our sin, and we become his righteousness. *"For He made Him who knew no sin to be sin for us, that we might become the righteousness of God in Him."* (2 Corinthians 5:21 NKJV) This is the message of reconciliation.

Reconciliation has several significant connotations. It is most significantly an exchange where two things change places, as would happen in a purchase. The money and the merchandise change place. It can mean buying something back or exchanging two things of equal value.[7]

---

[7] NT:2644, (from Thayer's Greek Lexicon, Electronic Database. Copyright © 2000, 2003, 2006 by Biblesoft, Inc. All rights reserved.)

Paul's gospel required that the Good News cover the Scriptural account of what happened on the Cross, in the grave, and through the resurrection. The reason it is crucial that one hear and believe each of these aspects of Jesus' finished work is that there is a very definite aspect of reconciliation (exchange) that has to be experienced in each of these areas if one is to live in total victory.

In 2 Corinthians 5:17-21, the Apostle Paul presents our call to be ambassadors of Christ. As such, our primary responsibility is to proclaim the message of reconciliation and to entice mankind to participate in this exchange!

All ministry, whether developing our own hearts, leading others to Jesus, healing, counseling, or conquering sin, is based on reconciliation! Anything that does not lead the believer to put off the old man and put on Christ is not based on the Cross. The failure of most ministry is the dependence on secular application, but not on the finished work of Jesus. Using biblical terminology does not mean the ministry is biblical.

The first two foundational doctrines, repentance of dead works and faith in God, are the two essential factors that must be present if we are to enter into this exchange. Reconciliation is based totally on what Jesus did, totally independent of our works or sacrifices.

From this point forward, each new doctrine is a benefit we share with Christ based on entering into the exchange. The doctrine of baptisms, laying on of hands, resurrection from the dead, and eternal judgment can only be grasped when we see how Jesus Himself fulfilled all that is required to participate. We share in the experience Jesus has already accomplished. He is the source; he gets all the glory!

The previous six doctrines lead us to the ultimate doctrine that becomes the cornerstone for all we receive from God: Jesus, our righteousness.

In a very subtle manner, laying on of hands is the foundational and introductory level of the exchange in personal ministry. All ministry, whether from the pulpit or on the street corner, must always lead the hearer to enter into the exchange, leaving their weaknesses, frailties, and sins with him on the Cross and abiding in him as the resurrected Lord!

16. Laying on of Hands in Scripture

As you read through this and think about these things, I hope that you are allowing the Holy Spirit to work in your heart. The goal of this book is not just to add information to your head but rather to change the quality of your life. When we take the time to invest in our hearts and to lay this foundation of the New Covenant, everything will change.

Let's look again at Hebrews 6:1-2 NKJV:

> *Therefore, leaving the discussion of the elementary principles of Christ, let us go on to perfection, (maturity) not laying again the foundation of repentance from dead works and of faith toward God, of the doctrine of baptisms, of laying on of hands....*

It says that we are to build from a foundation of repentance from dead works, from faith in God, and from a doctrine of baptisms and the laying on of hands. During the last chapter, we discussed the different baptisms under this New Covenant. We talked about being baptized by the Spirit into the body of Christ and how that takes place at the New Birth. We talked about baptism in water, what that implies, and how when water baptism is done in faith, it becomes a life-giving power in our lives. Lastly, we talked about the baptism by Jesus into the Holy Spirit as something distinctly different from being born-again, which is when the Holy Spirit initially comes into us.

The Holy Spirit coming upon us is for the purpose of empowerment for ministry. This leads to the fourth foundational doctrine, the laying on of hands. Please always remember, that much like baptism in water, unless it is connected by faith, any ceremony will remain lifeless, powerless, and just a tradition. Power is released when obedience is joined to faith.

"For indeed the gospel was preached to us as well as to them; but the word which they heard did not profit them, not being mixed with faith in those who heard it." (Hebrews 4:2 NKJV)

All things are possible for those who believe. Scripture describes the purpose of the laying on of hands in many places, but for practical purposes, it is always tied to the realm of personal ministry. Every believer is called to a life of ministry. Ministry is not just for the clergy; ministry is for every believer.

In the past, there has been a separation between the clergy and the laity that created an "us versus them" mentality. We often looked at the man or woman of God as the person that was anointed by God to minister to us and to represent God. I praise God that these things are changing. We know now that every believer is called to minister, every believer has access to the throne of grace, and every believer is anointed by the anointing of Jesus to minister the Gospel.

As an evangelist who has had the opportunity to travel the world, one thing that I still see in many nations is the concept that if we need something from God, we have to go through a mediator or through a man of God. But consider this: because we have right standing and personal rapport with God, we can go directly to him through his son. It is because of an Old Covenant mindset that we have doctrines of impartation, special anointing, and spiritual covering.

> **PEOPLE CHASE THE MAN OF GOD BECAUSE THEY BELIEVE THAT HE HAS SOMETHING THAT THEY DO NOT.**

People chase the man of God because they believe that he has something that they do not. That is not the Gospel. It is a form of Gnosticism that has people seeking special revelation, special anointing, and special power instead of believing that they already have all those things through the finished work of Jesus Christ. This was one of the reasons that the apostle Paul wrote the book of Colossians- to show believers in Colossi that they were already complete in Christ.

They did not lack anything. They were already anointed. They already had power over the devil, and they already had a new nature. They were complete in Him.

So instead of running to different people and trying to appropriate a special anointing or a special impartation, seek Jesus directly. Paul was trying to help the Colossians become established in who they were in Christ. You, too, are anointed, and you are complete in Christ. That said, when we talk about the laying on of hands, we are not talking about you getting something that you don't have. We're talking about the realm and understanding in which every one of us is called, equipped, and anointed by God to minister.

Examples from the Bible

Let's look at what the Bible says about this subject. In the Old Testament, the laying on of hands was used at different times and in different ways. One of the main ways it was used was when a priest or a Levite was ordained into the priesthood to serve. When Moses ordained Aaron and his sons to minister, one of the ceremonies began with an animal sacrifice. They then took the blood and touched it to the right ear and the right thumb. This represented having ears to hear. Their ears had been consecrated by the blood to hear the voice of God. They then touched the blood to the thumbs and the toes. This represented consecration for all that they did and all places that they went. Lastly, they laid hands on the priest. In this case, Moses laid hands on Aaron to consecrate him into the ministry.

The same idea took place when Moses consecrated Joshua into ministry. It was done through the laying on of hands. In the Old Testament, the laying on of hands was a sign of being consecrated to minister on behalf of God to the people.

When we transition over into the New Testament, we see that the main instances in the Gospels where it talks about the laying on of hands take place in Jesus' ministry to the sick. Jesus laid hands on the sick, representing the power of God that was in him, flowing into that sick person and them being healed.

And behold, one of the rulers of the synagogue came, Jairus by name. And when he saw Him, he fell at His feet and begged Him earnestly, saying, "My little daughter lies at the point of death. Come and lay Your hands on her, that she may be healed, and she will live. (Mark 5:22-23 NKJV)

> YOU DON'T HAVE TO LAY HANDS ON SOMEONE IN ORDER TO SEE THEM HEALED.

As I travel the world, especially in cultures sensitive and connected to the spiritual realm, there is a great deal superstition around the laying on of hands. I want you to know that you don't have to lay hands on someone in order to see them healed. Jesus also spoke the Word and received the same results. The apostles spoke the Word, and people were healed.

I remember hearing about TL Osborn. Back in the 1960s, he discovered that when he taught and preached the Word of God, it would bring people to a place where they could actually receive the Word for themselves. As a result, faith would come alive, and they would receive their miracle without hands being laid on them.

We know that Romans 10:17 says, *"Faith comes by hearing and hearing by the word of God."* The Word referred to by Paul was not the Bible as a whole, but more specifically, the Good News of the Gospel of Peace. When the Good News is proclaimed, the result will be trust in the goodness and faithfulness of God. In that atmosphere, miracles manifest.

Prior to the time of TL Osborn, the traditional way for healing evangelists to minister to the sick was to line people up and go down the line, laying on hands and praying for each individual person. Sometimes they would pray all night long.

Yes, it is scriptural to lay hands on the sick. Jesus laid hands on the sick. The apostles laid hands on the sick. However, you will not always be able to lay hands on every person. I believe there is a better way, which is getting people to believe and stand on the Word of God for themselves. When we help people to move into faith and stand on the Word for themselves, they will receive from God through their own belief and not that of someone else. The secret is not in the laying on of hands but in the significance of the power of God coming into you personally.

Laying on of hands for ordination into the ministry is another biblical use of the laying on of hands that Paul followed.

"Therefore, I remind you to stir up the gift of God which is in you through the laying on of my hands." (2 Timothy 1:6 NKJV)

Something took place, some sort of activation or a stirring up happening when Paul laid hands on Timothy. I believe that the gifts of the Spirit come into us through the infilling of the Holy Spirit, but I believe that the laying on of hands can be a way that we stir up or activate the gifts of God, which are already within us. The focus must not be on receiving something we do not have but rather on stirring up what we do have.

Paul told Timothy to stir up the gifts of God, which are in you. The gifts of God are in you, but you need to stir them up. Another translation says, *"fan into flame."* We can stir the gifts of God up, and one way this is done is through the laying on of hands.

Laying on of hands, according to scripture, is a type of endorsement. Moses, when he commissioned Joshua as his successor, endorsed him by the laying on the hands. Ordination into the ministry in the New Testament was also done through the laying on of hands.

In the book of Acts, the baptism of the Holy Spirit often took place in people's lives through the laying on of hands.

> *And it happened, while Apollos was at Corinth, that Paul, having passed through the upper regions, came to Ephesus. And finding some disciples he said to them, "Did you receive the Holy Spirit when you believed?" So, they said to him, "We have not so much as heard whether there is a Holy Spirit." And he said to them, "Into what then were you baptized?" So, they said, "Into John's baptism." Then Paul said, "John baptized with a baptism of repentance, saying to the people that they should believe on Him who would come after him, that is, on Christ Jesus." When they heard this, they were baptized in the name of the Lord Jesus. And when Paul had laid hands on them, the Holy Spirit came upon them, and they spoke with tongues and prophesied."* (Acts 19:1-6 NKJV)

Therefore, there must be a reality beyond this ceremony of the laying on of hands, or all it symbolizes is lifeless tradition. When combined with faith, it becomes a point of contact with the reality of the Gospel and the present work of the Holy Spirit in and through us. When God anointed Jesus, it says that the Holy Spirit came upon him, and he began to minister the Gospel in power.

Chapter Questions

1. What is the laying on of hands referring to in scripture?
2. Explain how ceremonies are powerless unless they are combined with faith.

17. Ministering in Power

When God anointed Jesus, the Bible says that the Holy Spirit came upon him and that he began to minister the Gospel in power. When God lays hands on us through the infilling of the Holy Spirit, we should begin to minister out of an overflow of God's power and anointing. This laying on of hands refers to the realm of personal ministry that belongs to every believer.

When hands are laid on an individual, we should remember first that God laid hands on Jesus, and he imparted to him all of our sin. God imparted to Jesus the punishment that we deserve, thus setting us free from the consequences and condemnation of sin and qualifying us for all the blessings God planned for mankind. Incredible! Think about that for a moment. God laid the sins of the world on Jesus Christ, who became our sin. Under the Old Covenant, the priest would lay hands on a sheep or a goat. This was symbolic of the sins of that person or nation being imparted to the animal. The goat was punished and judged so that the worshiper could go free from judgment. Under the New Covenant, the entirety of the sins of the world were laid upon Jesus, and he received the consequences that we deserve.

As a result, God can lay his hand of blessing on us and impart all the blessings that Jesus Christ obtained through his death, burial, and resurrection. Therefore, we receive the empowerment that Jesus had, and we begin to live out of that overflow of the Spirit.

Jesus, the man

It is crucial that we remember that everything that Jesus did, he did as a man who was empowered by the Holy Spirit. He was a man who allowed the Holy Spirit to flow and operate through him. Our hope of victory, our hope of success in ministry, and our perspective must be in recognizing the humanity of Jesus.

Philippians says:

> *Let this mind be in you which was also in Christ Jesus, who, being in the form of God, did not consider it robbery to be equal with God, but made Himself of no reputation, taking the form of a bondservant, and coming in the likeness of men.* (Philippians 2:5-7 NKJV)

This verse says Jesus took upon himself the nature of a servant, coming in our likeness. He came to our level so that he could restore us back to his. Every miracle that Jesus did, every time he placed his hands on the sick, every miracle of healing, every time he loved the unlovable or restored broken people, he was operating as a man in right relationship with God, yielded to the Holy Spirit.

In our own personal ministry, we can do the same things Jesus did during his earthly walk. We are operating as a person full of the Holy Spirit and fully yielded to grace.

"So, Jesus said to them again, 'Peace to you! As the Father has sent Me, I also send you'. And when He had said this, He breathed on them, and said to them, 'Receive the Holy Spirit'". (John 20:21-22 NKJV)

After Jesus rose from the dead, he commissioned and sent his disciples out, saying, *"As the father sent me, I also send you."* The same anointing, the same power, the same presence that Jesus had, and the same commissioning that Jesus operated from is what God gives us in Christ.

Greater works

"Most assuredly, I say to you, he who believes in Me, the works that I do he will do also; and greater works than these he will do, because I go to My Father." (John 14:12 NKJV)

We have the opportunity to do the same works that Jesus Christ did. We have this empowerment because Jesus went to the Father, and then the Holy Spirit came. What that implies is that we can lay hands on the sick, and we can see them healed. We can set people free. We can proclaim freedom to the captives, recovery of sight to the blind, healing for the lame, and cleansing for lepers. I have seen it! Signs and wonders still follow the preaching of the Gospel.

I've seen all of these things, not because of my great faith or special anointing, but because I obeyed the Word of God and went. TL Osborn would constantly say, *"I don't have anything you don't have. I don't have any special anointing or gifts. I've got the Holy Spirit and I've got the Word of God."*

Friends, you are called to minister in the same power and same anointing that Jesus Christ had and operated under. You don't need a special anointing. You have the anointing of Jesus. If it was good enough for Jesus, you don't need to run after some man of God for them to lay hands on you. You have the anointing of Jesus, and those things can be stirred up in you, but you must operate in faith. You must step out and begin to trust Christ in you.

> YOU ARE CALLED TO MINISTER IN THE SAME POWER AND SAME ANOINTING THAT JESUS CHRIST HAD AND OPERATED UNDER.

> *And He said to them, 'Go into all the world and preach the gospel to every creature... And these signs will follow those who believe: In My name they will cast out demons; they will speak with new tongues; they will take up serpents; and if they drink anything deadly, it will by no means hurt them; they will lay hands on the sick, and they will recover'... So then, after the Lord had spoken to them, He was received up into heaven, and sat down at the right hand of God. And they went out and preached everywhere, the Lord working with them and confirming the word through the accompanying signs.* (Mark 16:15-20 NKJV)

Jesus said to go into all the world and preach the Gospel, and then he said, "…and these signs will follow those who believe." If you are a believer, you should expect God to be ministering through you through signs, wonders, and miracles.

When Jesus says, "*In my name,*" what does he mean? He means that as his representative, and in his place, Jesus was giving us power of attorney-the power to act in his name. I remember back when I purchased my first house. I was in New Zealand at the time, so I created a legally binding document giving my father power of attorney. What that meant was that he could make business transactions in my name, just as if I was there. He was given the authority to use my name. So what Jesus is saying now is that, as my representative, because I'm not there, I give you the power to use my name and to do business in my place. This includes healing the sick and casting out demons using his authority and power.

> **DEMONS WON'T BE AN ISSUE BECAUSE JESUS DEFEATED ALL RULE, ALL POWER, ALL AUTHORITY, AND ALL THE DOMINION OF DARKNESS.**

This is an awesome revelation right here. Jesus says that "*In my name, you will cast out de*mons." Demons won't be an issue because Jesus defeated all rule, all power, all authority, and all the dominion of darkness. He defeated them on the Cross. Therefore, in his name, which is the name above all names, we can deal with demons (and any other issues).

You have read the verse that says, "*They will speak in new tongues.*" That refers to the baptism of the Holy Spirit. "*They shall take up serpents.*" He's not talking about some traditions that take place in different Pentecostal groups. What he is referring to is that we will have protection against deadly creatures, deadly viruses, and any other deadly things that come against us as we take his Gospel to the world. That goes right along with the verse that says, "*If they drink anything deadly, it will by no means hurt them.*"

Think of the apostle Paul. When he was shipwrecked on the island of Malta, as he was picking up sticks for the fire, a deadly serpent was driven out by the heat. It attached itself to Paul, and he just shook it off into the fire and suffered no ill effects. The locals expected him to fall over dead at any moment, but he shook it off, and he suffered no ill effects. When you go to the world with the Gospel, you will experience opportunities where you are going to have to trust God. Jesus is giving a promise of protection against illness, sickness, and demonic attacks. We are promised that as we focus on taking the Gospel to the world, we can have supernatural protection against harm.

Healing in the early church

Jesus makes available a promise of protection, a promise of authority over demons, and a promise of Holy Spirit baptism. Lastly, he says, we *"will lay hands on the sick and they will recover."*

This was normal for the operation of the early church. This was the message of healing that the early church believed. They practiced laying on of hands and anointing the sick with oil, as described in James, chapter five.

> *Is anyone among you sick? Let him call for the elders of the church, and let them pray over him, anointing him with oil in the name of the Lord. And the prayer of faith will save the sick, and the Lord will raise him up.* (James 5:14-15 NKJV)

If you were sick in the early church, they would lay hands on you, or they would anoint you with oil and then expect healing. Healing has always been God's will. Healing has always been provided in scripture. God doesn't choose to heal one and not another. God is consistent. His promises are true and available for everyone who will believe them. The way that the New Testament believers of the early church exercised faith for healing was through the laying on of hands, and the sick were healed.

Therefore, the Apostle Paul, when talking about the New Covenant doctrine of the laying on of hands, was referring to the realm of personal ministry to which every believer is called to live in and operate from. He was talking about a place where we believe that we have been anointed and have been called by God to operate in faith. This is not something that we need to chase after. It is something that God has already given believers. We are anointed and commissioned.

Chapter Questions

1. Why is the humanity of Jesus our hope for victory in life and ministry?

2. Why is it important that every believer be active in evangelism and ministry?

18. Releasing Your Faith

In the book of Philemon, Paul gives us one of the greatest personal benefits gained from living in this realm of personal ministry.

"I pray that the sharing of your faith may become effective for the full knowledge of every good thing that is in us for the sake of Christ." (Philemon 1:6 ESV)

This verse tells us that one of the benefits of effectively and actively sharing our faith is that we will begin to understand everything that we have through Jesus' finished work. As we minister to others, we will begin to receive an awareness of every good thing that we have in Jesus Christ. Ministry is a place where we can apply what we know by discipling and communicating the Gospel with others. As we do this, it brings a greater awareness of who we are in Jesus Christ.

Allow me to share this verse from the Amplified translation.

That the participation in and sharing of your faith may produce and promote full recognition and appreciation and understanding and precise knowledge of every good [thing] that is ours in [our identification with] Christ Jesus [and unto His glory. (Philemon 1:6 AMP)

The most mature Christians have developed a habit of sharing their faith. This is a sign of maturity and that the information has gone from the head to the heart. When we begin to actively participate in the Gospel, changes begin to occur. When we see ourselves as ministers of the Gospel, share our faith and lay hands on the sick, and engage the opportunities that God gives us, we move into a place of maturity and personal application as disciples and not just as converts.

The most joyful Christians are the ones who have made a habit of sharing their faith. They see and engage in the opportunities that God has given them. I have many stories of going through my daily duties and being at the right place and the right time to influence someone's life for good.

On one occasion, when I was traveling and sitting in the airport, waiting for my ride to come, an older man with a brace on his knee sat down next to me. I simply asked him if I could pray for him. He looked at me kind of strangely, and I assured him that I was not weird but that I had a relationship with a God who heals people's bodies as well as their hearts. He allowed me to go ahead and pray for him. I placed my hand on his shoulder, and I said, *"Father, would you show this man that you love him? I ask you to heal him right now."* I prayed a very simple prayer, and all of a sudden, the power of God was shown, and his knee healed. He began to move his knee and to laugh. I said that this is how much God cares for you. The man became tremendously grateful and joyful. A seed was planted in that moment of the goodness of God.

Build faith into people first

God cares about the little things in our life. The above testimony was me just being available to access God's ability. It was me seeing myself as being anointed and placed in a position to demonstrate the Gospel. I believe that is what Paul was talking about when he mentioned laying on of hands as a New Covenant foundational doctrine. He was referring, first of all, to what took place when God laid his hands on Jesus and imparted our sins to him. Next, he was referring to how, through the Holy Spirit, God imparts to us his nature, his anointing, and the use of his name. Our part is to move out of our comfort zone and move into the power and demonstration of the Gospel.

"And as you go, preach, saying, 'The Kingdom of heaven is at hand. Heal the sick, cleanse the lepers, raise the dead, cast out demons. Freely you have received, freely give'". (Matthew 10:7-9 NKJV)

Jesus is saying that freely you have received, now freely give. We need to come to a place where ministering is an overflow of the love that God has freely given to us. We need to become comfortable with ministering the Gospel to people. Here is a key principle to keep in mind: As you begin a lifestyle of ministry, always share the Word with people first. Often, we are quick to want to pray and lay hands on someone, but they may need to receive the Word first.

Romans 10:17 NKJV says, *"Faith comes by hearing, and hearing by the word of God."* If we take the time to actually share the Word with people, faith will come into their hearts.

God confirms his Word. He doesn't confirm us or our word. He is not confirming our ministry. He's confirming the Word of the Gospel. If you take the time to invest in people with the Word of God, you will see many more people healed than if you just lay hands on them and pray for healing.

IF YOU TAKE THE TIME TO INVEST IN PEOPLE WITH THE WORD OF GOD, YOU WILL SEE MANY MORE PEOPLE HEALED THAN IF YOU JUST LAY HANDS ON THEM AND PRAY FOR HEALING.

Many times, we also need to lead people in the prayer of faith. James chapter five says the prayer of faith will heal the sick. We are to pray in faith, but sometimes we need to help people move into a place of faith where they can receive the Word of God for themselves.

In ministering to people, it is also important that we help them to exercise their faith. People are the ones that have authority over their situations. We can lay hands on and pray for people, but it is even better when we actually lead people to exercise their own faith over their own sickness. After that, you can follow up by laying hands on them and calling them healed. Just speak what the Word of God says and expect healing to manifest in them.

So how do you start? If all you receive from this reading is mere information, then you're not actually going to see it working in your life. In every ceremony or tradition, we must exercise faith. As in the ceremony of baptism, we have to exercise faith for it to become powerful in our lives. It is the same with this doctrine of the laying on of hands. Apply faith to where you realize you have been anointed. Apply it to where you have been called and consecrated by God to live. Do this and experience an incredible supernatural life.

When you begin to walk out your faith daily, seeing the opportunities, sooner or later, you will acquire a greater understanding of Christ in you. You will come to a deeper maturity level and experience the joy of the Lord because you are living out your faith in real life.

Chapter Questions

1. What is some practical advice on leading people in healing prayer that you have learned? How can you apply these principles?

2. Are you active in sharing your faith? Why or why not? What are some steps you can take to make it a lifestyle?

For further reading, we recommend the books ***Supernatural Ministry***, by Dr. Jim Richards and ***Simply Gospel***, by Nathan Tanner.

Section 7 Resurrection From The Dead

Introduction

Dr. Jim Richards

The resurrection of the dead is the one undeniable truth that validates Jesus' claims of identity and his supremacy to any who would ever claim to be deity.

Both John and Paul identify Jesus as the firstborn from the dead. Unless we qualify this statement, it can be proven to be untrue. Plus, as it stands, it loses its importance and significance in the doctrine of the Covenant! Jesus absolutely was not the first person to ever be raised from the dead. There had been people raised from the dead in the Old Testament! There had been people raised from the dead under his own earthly ministry. So, how could He claim to be the "firstborn from the dead?"

Jesus was not the firstborn from physical death. He was, however, the firstborn to be resurrected from the death of sin! It is that resurrection that provides us with the greatest promise. It is that resurrection wherein we enter into the exchange right now in this life.

On the Cross, Jesus literally became our sin. By becoming our sin, he freed us from our sin nature. Then by becoming our sin, he faced all the consequences that we would have had to face and endure if we had died in that sin. Because he became our sin, he was alienated from God. In his death, he entered into the realm of Hades used to hold those who died in sin. This would have been our eternal abode had he not paid this price for us.[8]

---
8   For a more detailed look into what happened while Jesus was

In the grave, he had become our sin. Therefore it was our sin that held him in death. For him to be raised from the dead, he had to specifically conquer our sin. Jonah chapter two provides one of the most graphic depictions of the battle Jesus fought to conquer our sin.

Jesus had numerous Scriptures that stated his eternal identity, but he was trapped in death in our identity! But he believed what God said about him and his eternal reign; in other words, he operated faith in God's view and opinion, even though his personal experience offered no hope!

> RESURRECTION POWER IS VAST; THERE IS PROBABLY NO END TO WHAT IS AVAILABLE TO US WHEN WE YIELD TO IT.

Jesus believed God and was raised up from the death of sin unto a righteous life. When we jointly share in Jesus' resurrection, the Apostle Paul explains that we experience resurrection power right now in this life. Resurrection power is vast; there is probably no end to what is available to us when we yield to it. But the most immediate benefit is the power to rise up out of temptation and sin and step into resurrection life now!

Obviously, the eternal value of resurrection from death is the most significant. It will be the final reconciliation of sin, which introduced death into our world.

It is important that the new believer be introduced to the concept of being raised up in newness of life at salvation. This is the beginning of eternal life. This is the time when we are passed from death to life. (John 5:24) Understanding that we have already been raised up prepares the believer to see life from the eternal perspective.

Knowing that we already participate in resurrection life delivers us from the illusion that this temporary existence is actually life. This brings to life the realization that we are crucified with Christ, we are dead to sin, and yes, we are the righteousness of God in Christ! Eternal realities are a fantasy to the believer who does not realize he or she has already begun to participate in resurrection life!

---

dead, check our Three Days That Changed the World

19. The Centrality of the Resurrection

A New Covenant Christ-centered belief system provides a foundation for everything that we believe and the way that we interpret scripture. God has given us several safety nets in scripture to ensure that our belief system and foundation stay firm, regardless of what happens in life.

The first safety net is the Gospels, the first four books of the New Testament. These reveal the life and the ministry of Jesus. What did he display? What did he show us about God? What was the interpretation that Jesus had about the nature and character of God? Remember that Jesus said, *"If you've seen me, you've seen the Father."* Therefore, if what we know about God does not pass through the interpretation of how Jesus revealed the Father, we may then find that much of what we believe about God is just not true.

The second is the death, burial, and resurrection of Jesus and the finished work of the Cross. If, in our reading of scripture, we come across something in scripture that appears to not be consistent with Jesus and what he accomplished through his death, burial, and resurrection, then we know that something is not right in our hearing or interpretation. For example, what if a preacher comes to you and says that if you don't give your tithes and offerings to the church, you will come under a curse? If you truly understand the finished work of the Cross, you will realize that the preacher is speaking of God from an Old Testament perspective. How do we know that for a fact? Because Galatians 3:13 NKJV says, *"Christ has redeemed us from the curse of the law, having become a curse for us.*" Everything that we understand about God and the Gospel must pass through the test of the finished work of the Cross.

The third safety net is found in the six foundational doctrines of the New Covenant, as described in Hebrews chapter six. There are two specific doctrines, the fifth and the sixth, that are pivotal to our understanding. The fifth doctrine is the teaching of the resurrection from the dead, and the sixth is the doctrine of eternal judgment. The doctrine of the resurrection from the dead was so important to the Apostle Paul that it was included in the six foundational doctrines of the New Covenant. These last two doctrines, the resurrection from the dead and eternal judgment, look forward into the future that will take place when Christ returns. They also strongly influence the quality of the Christian life that you are living now. For the believer, resurrection life is both past, present, and future.

> TO DIE WITHOUT CHRIST MEANS YOU HAVE LOST EVERYTHING. TO DIE WITH CHRIST MEANS THAT YOU ARE SIMPLY TRANSITIONING INTO THE NEXT SEASON WITH GOD.

Understanding the resurrection from the dead is a central piece of the Gospel, which gives hope for both the present and the future. As a younger evangelist, I used to emphasize how Jesus saves us from hell and gives us the promise of heaven. As time went on and I grew in my understanding of the goodness and grace of God and determined to focus on what Christ brings into our lives now. I continue to do this because I believe that God wants to give us an incredible quality of life now. He wants to bring the blessings of the Kingdom into our day-to-day lives. However, that does not change the fact that Jesus Christ gives us hope for the future. To die without Christ means you have lost everything. To die with Christ means that you are simply transitioning into the next season with God. The most important thing is our relationship with God. The Gospel gives us hope, not only for the here and now but also for the future.

Hebrews 12:28 NKJV says, *"Therefore, since we are receiving a Kingdom that cannot be shaken, let us have grace, by which we may serve God acceptably with reverence and godly fear."*

When we have a view of the Kingdom as not just in the future but also in the present, we have our understanding of the Kingdom aligned correctly. This will give us the grace to serve God with reverence and godly fear. We need an eternal perspective. We need the promises working in our life now, and we also need that hope of eternity. The resurrection from the dead is a doctrine that we must not only understand intellectually, but it must also be part of the faith foundation that is working in our lives.

The resurrection of Jesus

The resurrection of Jesus Christ is the central piece of the Gospel. Without the resurrection, all we have is a dead martyr. As you go through the book of Acts, you will see over and over again that the heart of the message that the apostles preached centered around not only Christ crucified but on Christ resurrected. Why? Because the resurrection is proof that what we have is different from all other religions. It is true that the resurrection of Jesus Christ is proof that Jesus is the Son of God, but it is also proof that one day we will be raised up with him.

There have always been those who denied the resurrection. From the days of Jesus and the apostles, even up to today, there are those who deny the resurrection. The main religious group that denied the resurrection in the time of Jesus was that of the Sadducees. You may remember Jesus was always arguing with the Pharisees, Sadducees, and other teachers of the law. The Sadducees were a group that denied the supernatural. They denied the reality of angels and demons, and they also denied that there was a future resurrection. They believed that what we had in this life was all there was, that a person came from the dirt and would return to dirt. That is a sad way to live, and that's why the Sadducees were without hope in an afterlife.

To not have any hope for the future is a dark way to live. The Gospel declares that the resurrection of Jesus Christ is proof that one day we will be resurrected. Death is never easy, but the resurrection of Jesus Christ is our guarantee that there is more to this life than this short time averaging 60 to 90 years. Our lifetime is a drop in the bucket compared to eternity. There is an eternal reality. When we have the hope of the resurrection, it gives us stability and hope for the future.

The resurrection also removes the fear of death. More than any other thing, people fear death. The reason that we fear death is that we don't know what the future holds. Human beings, by nature, are afraid of the unknown. Most people are afraid to step out into a business venture or a new path of education, largely because they have become comfortable with what is familiar. When we step out into the unknown, it is a scary prospect! God never wants us to approach life with uncertainty. He never wants us to look at the future with fear. The resurrection of Jesus is proof that we will one day be resurrected. It is proof that we will be raised up with Christ. This removes the fear of the unknown and the fear of death. We have hope, not only in this life but in the future.

Christ, the pioneer

Christ Jesus has pioneered every aspect of our redemption, including the resurrection from the dead. He is the captain, the forerunner, the pioneer of our eternal redemption reality. He paid the price on the Cross. He defeated death. He rose up in victory, and he also pioneered this aspect of eternal life and resurrection.

If there is no resurrection from the dead, then, as the apostle Paul said, *"We are more men to be pitied than anyone else."*

Let's look at 1 Corinthians 15:12-19 NKJV:

> *Now if Christ is preached that He has been raised from the dead, how do some among you say that there is no resurrection of the dead? But if there is no resurrection of the dead, then Christ is not risen. And if Christ is not risen, then our preaching is empty, and your faith is also empty. Yes, and we are found false witnesses of God because we have testified of God that He raised up Christ, whom He did not raise up—if in fact the dead do not rise. For if the dead do not rise, then Christ is not risen. And if Christ is not risen, your faith is futile; you are still in your sins! Then also those who have fallen asleep in Christ have perished. If in this life only we have hope in Christ, we are of all men the most pitiable.*

In 1 Corinthians chapter 15, the Apostle Paul begins to frame out the arguments that the foundation of the Gospel is the revelation that Jesus

Christ has been raised from the dead. If you remove the resurrection, you are left with a hopeless life, and the best you have is what you receive here in this life.

Paul goes on to say that if Christ has not been raised from the dead, then you are dead in your sins. The resurrection is the very heartbeat of the Gospel. It is the resurrection of Jesus Christ that sets all religions apart from biblical Christianity. I've traveled to Buddhist, Hindu, and Muslim nations. What makes Jesus Christ unique? It's not great teaching. It's not even the miracles. What makes biblical Christianity unique is the resurrection of Jesus Christ. Buddha, Mohammed, and Joseph Smith of the Mormons are all dead and still in the grave. There are actually shrines that you can visit and see to this day, but you can't visit and see the bones of Jesus because they are not there. Three days and three nights after Jesus died, he rose again from the dead. That is proof that he is the Son of God, that he is the way, the truth, and the life. It also is proof that he will receive us as his own and one day take us to be with him forever.

Chapter Questions

1. What separates the Gospel from all other religions?
2. What are some of the misunderstandings concerning the resurrection?

20. A Future Resurrection

When the Bible was written, there were two significant belief misconceptions that people were likely to fall into when it came to teachings about the resurrection. The Apostle Paul dealt with both of them in his epistles.

The first one was where people believed that the resurrection from the dead had already happened. They believed that it was past and that they had all been left behind- they had missed it. Paul debunked this at length in several of the epistles to ensure that his churches understood the truth. The other misconception was the belief that there wasn't going to be a resurrection. So, one said that the resurrection was passed, and the other said that there was no resurrection. We must be careful regarding what we believe about the resurrection, given that the Apostle Paul considered it so important that he actually included it in the foundations of faith.

The Bible is absolutely clear that there will be a resurrection of the righteous and of the wicked. It specifies that two distinct judgments will take place. The first is the Judgment Seat of Christ. 2 Corinthians 5:10 NKJV says, *"For we must all appear before the judgment seat of Christ, that each one may receive the things done in the body, according to what he has done, whether good or bad."*

When Paul talked about the Judgment Seat of Christ, he was talking about the event where believers would stand on judgment day and give an account of their lives. Religion would make us afraid of the Judgment Seat of Christ. Religion would make us become self-conscious and introspective. It creates an expectation of condemnation. I have even heard teachings of how God is going to play every bad thing that you have ever done on the heavenly big screen TV. Nothing could be further from the truth if you are a believer. By believing in him, a great exchange has taken place, and your judgment has already happened. You have already been judged as being righteous based on Jesus' sacrifice. Therefore, the Judgment seat of Christ is a place of receiving rewards. We will expound more upon this in the next section.

> THOSE WHOSE NAMES ARE NOT FOUND WRITTEN IN THE BOOK OF LIFE WILL BE THROWN INTO A LAKE OF FIRE.

For unbelievers, the Bible, in Revelation chapter 20, says that we will stand before the Great White Throne Judgment. This will be the judgment for the wicked and everyone that rejected the Gospel. At the resurrection of the wicked, the Bible tells us that the sea will give up the dead and that they will all come alive to stand before God to be judged. Those whose names are not found written in the Book of Life will be thrown into a lake of fire. The Bible teaches very clearly that there will be a resurrection of the righteous and the wicked, and we will all stand before God. I don't believe that believers will stand with unbelievers; it will be a different judgment. The Judgment Seat of Christ for believers is a place of rewards.

Where do you go when you die?

So, let's ask the question, what happens when a person dies? When a believer dies, they will go immediately to the presence of God in heaven. This is clearly taught in scripture. Many people have the idea that when a sinner dies, they go directly to the lake of fire. If you study scripture, the lake of fire is really only mentioned one time in Revelation chapter 20. It says that at the final judgment, Satan, and everyone who aligns himself with him, will be thrown into the lake of fire.

So where did people go in the past, and where do they go right now when they pass away? According to scripture and according to the teachings of Jesus, when the wicked died prior to Christ's finished work, they went to a place called Hades or a holding place. If you want to study this further,

A Future Resurrection

you can look at Luke chapter 16, which talks about the rich man and Lazarus. It says when both of them died, the rich man was thrown into Hades, and Lazarus, the poor God-fearing beggar, went to Abraham's bosom. According to this parable, there was a holding place where the wicked and the righteous went. This was before Jesus rose from the dead, and the wicked were waiting there.

When Jesus rose from the dead, he held captivity captive. He emptied Abraham's bosom, the place where the righteous had been waiting. This is where the Old Testament saints, Abraham, Isaac, Jacob, King David, the prophets, and the Old Testament saints were waiting in hope for the Messiah. Jesus came, and when he rose from the dead, he gathered up all of those saints, and he led them in his celebration train up to the Father in heaven. Jesus emptied Abraham's bosom. But according to scripture, it appears that the ungodly are still waiting for that final day of judgment.

At the end of the age, when Jesus Christ returns to the earth, he will return with the believers who have been in heaven, and he will meet up with the believers still on earth, where he will rule and reign. He will renew the earth. This is the fulfillment of the Gospel. Ultimately, the goal of Christ is that he would rule and reign on the earth. The goal of the Gospel is not just people going to heaven when they die. The goal of the Gospel is that one day, heaven and earth would become one in Jesus Christ, and he would rule on the earth as King of Kings and Lord of Lords for all eternity.

This gives us hope, imparts peace, and gives us perspective.

"We are confident, yes, well pleased rather to be absent from the body and to be present with the Lord." (2 Corinthians 5:8 NKJV)

Chapter Questions

1. What happens for believers and unbelievers after the resurrection? What does Christ's resurrection provide for you now?
2. What took place through Christ's resurrection?

21. Eternal Life Now

Let's examine this topic a little further. I don't believe that the doctrine of resurrection is limited to just a future resurrection. I believe that God has resurrection life for us right now.

"And this is eternal life, that they may know You, the only true God, and Jesus Christ whom You have sent." (John 17:3 NKJV)

Jesus very clearly says that eternal life is not just heaven for us when we die but that eternal life begins the moment we give our lives to him. The moment we say yes and believe the Gospel, we cross over from death into the realm called eternal life. It shall never end.

We are eternal beings. God made us this way, and in a very real way, we are never going to die. We are going to live forever. Our spirits will go on living with the Lord, and then one day, we will have the resurrection of our bodies. However, God wants us to experience his eternal quality of life here and now. He wants us to experience the benefits of the Kingdom —the benefits of heaven here during our life on this earth.

The foundation of the doctrine of resurrection life is not only for the future but also for the present. When the New Testament uses the word "life," it uses the Greek word "Zoe." What this word literally means is *"the quality of life possessed by the one who gives it."* God has a quality of life, and he gives it to the person who believes on Jesus. We can experience the eternal quality of life that God lives and experiences.

Listen to these words:

> *Therefore I also, after I heard of your faith in the Lord Jesus and your love for all the saints, do not cease to give thanks for you, making mention of you in my prayers: that the God of our Lord Jesus Christ, the Father of glory, may give to you the spirit of wisdom and revelation in the knowledge of Him, the eyes of your understanding being enlightened; that you may know what is the hope of His calling, what are the riches of the glory of His inheritance in the saints, and what is the exceeding greatness of His power toward us who believe, according to the working of His mighty power.* (Ephesians 1:15-19 NKJV)

God wants us to have wisdom and revelation in the knowledge of him. True wisdom and revelation are found in Christ. They are not found in how much we know but rather found in knowing Jesus. Jesus is the wisdom of God; he reveals the logic of God. Paul prays that *"the Father of glory would give us the spirit of wisdom and revelation in the knowledge of him."* He explains further by praying that *"the eyes of your understanding would be enlightened."* One translation says the *"eyes of our hearts"* would be enlightened so that we can see Christ as he is and see ourselves as we really are in Christ.

He then goes on to pray for three different things that you should see. He first prays for the eyes of our understanding to be enlightened so that we may know the *"hope of his calling."* Notice he doesn't say the *"hope of your calling."* He is not talking about our individual calling. He is talking about getting a revelation of the calling of Christ, what God accomplished through Christ, and what God has called Christ to be for us in all things. God has called Christ to be the center of everything. Jesus is Lord. He is the one that God the Father has appointed to judge the world. He prays that you would know the hope of his calling.

Next, he prays for us to know *"what are the riches of the glory of His inheritance in the saints."* Again, he is not referring to our personal inheritance. He is talking about the inheritance of Christ. Did you know that Jesus Christ, through his death and resurrection, received an inheritance from the Father? That inheritance includes eternal life. It also includes every promise of God. We need revelation from God to understand Jesus' inheritance because we participate in that inheritance through faith in Jesus Christ.

Lastly, he prays for us to know the "*exceeding greatness of his power towards us who believe.*" The Apostle Paul wants believers to know by revelation, through having the eyes of our hearts enlightened:

What is the exceeding greatness of His power toward us who believe, according to the working of His mighty power which He worked in Christ when He raised Him from the dead and seated Him at His right hand in the heavenly places, far above all principality and power and might and dominion, and every name that is named, not only in this age but also in that which is to come. (Ephesians 1:19-22 NKJV)

We need revelation to understand the power of God, which is working in us and flowing through us. It is the same resurrection power and resurrection life that God used to raise Jesus from the dead. It says that he raised him from the dead and seated him at his right hand in the heavenly realms, far above all power and authority, might and dominion, and every name that is named. This is not only in this age but also in the age to come. That is a lot of resurrection power. This is resurrection life- the life and power of God that he demonstrated through the resurrection of Jesus. The same power is working on the inside of us. That same power is qualifying us and giving us the ability to walk out the promises of God.

An absolute victory

Resurrection life is not only for the future but also for us here and now. We can operate in that same power and authority. Jesus stripped the devil of all dominion when he rose from the dead. He stripped the devil of all his accusations against us. Jesus is Lord of all. Therefore, we are not subject to any demonic power as we participate in Christ's victory. We have the privilege to live as absolute conquerors, not only in the far future but here and now; we can experience the resurrection power of God.

Paul, in talking about the power of the Cross, said,

Having wiped out the handwriting of requirements that was against us, which was contrary to us. And He has taken it out of the way, having nailed it to the cross. Having disarmed principalities and powers, He made a public spectacle of them, triumphing over them in it. (Colossians 2:14-15 NKJV)

In Roman times, which was in Paul's time, an enemy king who terrorized another kingdom, after victory was gained, would take that enemy king and bring him back to Rome. The first thing they would do was humiliate him by stripping him naked. They would then march him through the streets of the city as the citizens would mock him and spit on him.

This was done as a sign to the people that this king that used to terrorize them, this king that used to strike fear into the hearts of the people, had lost all of his power. He had lost his ability to inflict fear. They would then march him through the streets and into the central square. Normally they would cut off his big toes and his thumbs. This was a sign that he could no longer carry a sword and no longer run into battle. After that, they would execute him.

Paul was describing a triumphal procession where an enemy king was being marched as a public spectacle through the streets of Rome. He was being declared powerless to inflict fear into people's lives. Now, through the Cross, that is exactly what Jesus Christ did to every demonic power. He stripped them of their ability and power to accuse us before God. The accusations of the law were nailed to the Cross. The devil has no power to accuse us before God any longer. The power of accusation, the power of fear and of bondage, has been destroyed forever. Now you and I can participate in Christ's victory.

Friends, we have resurrection life now, as well as in the future. The Gospel gives us not only a sure foundation for the future and not only takes away the fear and uncertainty of death, but it also empowers us to live resurrection life right here and right now in this present world. This is the doctrine of the resurrection from the dead. Christ has risen from the dead, and we have a sure hope of a future resurrection, and as we wait, we participate in it.

Chapter Questions

1. What is a triumphal procession?
2. Did Jesus totally defeat Satan? If so, what does that mean for you?

For further study, please refer to *Satan Unmasked* by Dr Jim Richards.

Section 8 Eternal Judgment

Introduction

Dr. Jim Richards

Eternal Judgments

There is a great misunderstanding in the body of Christ about forgiveness. The general concept is forgiveness is God simply overlooking sin or just letting it go. In Exodus 34:17, God says He cannot hold a person innocent who is guilty of an offense. It would be a violation of his justice. If forgiveness was simply declaring a guilty person as innocent, then forgiveness would be nothing more than lying or a cover-up!

Judgment is not always negative. There are positive judgments as well as negative judgments! Judgment is declaring any act, whether internal or external, as good or evil. When Adam acquired the knowledge of good and evil, he became his own god. He evidently believed that this newfound capacity meant that if he judged something good, it was good.

This is at the heart of why the world hates God and does everything possible to convince itself that there is no God. If there is a Creator God, he would very definitely be the One who has the right to determine good and evil. Those who desire to fulfill their lusts must reject the thought of anyone other than themselves having the right to judge good and evil. Therefore, the human race today, more than ever, attempts to claim the right of self-judgment, calling good evil and evil good! Then they try to force their wicked, unjust judgments on society.

The doctrine of eternal judgment is where all of creation has to acknowledge God as Creator and Lord! He alone has the right to determine good and evil. When the veil of darkness and self-deceit is removed, then all will have to bow their knee in acknowledgment of his justice.

> WHEN WE ACKNOWLEDGE THE NEED FOR FORGIVENESS, WE ARE ENTERING INTO AN AGREEMENT WITH GOD CONCERNING OUR GUILTY VERDICT.

Before coming to Jesus, we abide in death, under the guilty verdict for all our sin. When we acknowledge the need for forgiveness, we are entering into an agreement with God concerning our guilty verdict. In essence, we are accepting God's judgment and penalty of death on that life. It isn't overlooked. It isn't covered. Jesus became our sin and paid the full consequence that we deserved.

If we have heard and believed the Gospel (which few new believers have), we learn that on the Cross, Jesus became our sin. In the grave, he paid the full penalty for our sin. Through the resurrection, a new righteous being is raised up. The one who committed all those sins accepted the guilty verdict and the penalty of death, which is considered fair and just.

Since the Scripture teaches that we cannot be penalized for the same crime twice (double jeopardy), and since we have accepted the judgment, we will never stand before God to account for those sins or any other aspect of our life outside of Jesus!

"Most assuredly, I say to you, he who hears My word and believes in Him who sent Me has everlasting life, and shall not come into judgment, but has passed from death into life." (John 5:24 NKJV)

There are two other judgments with which we should concern ourselves. The one that is most relevant for believers is called the Judgment Seat of Christ. This judgment is not to determine if we will spend eternity with God. It will, however, determine our eternal rewards.

"For we must all appear before the judgment seat of Christ, that each one may receive the things done in the body, according to what he has done, whether good or bad." (2 Corinthians 5:10)

Introduction

As we have learned, faith believes God is a rewarder. There are incredible benefits, fruit, and rewards for those who trust God. Good works, as opposed to dead works, are the fruit of faith and love. Additionally, there is the issue of our eternal inheritance, as sons and heirs, that must be resolved.

We will all appear before the judgment seat of Christ for the purpose of receiving rewards. According to 1 Corinthians 3:12-15, all our works will be tested by fire. Those works that are acceptable to him will be presented to him for his glory. We will get to see the eternal benefits of all we did in his name. Those things that are not worthy to present to our Lord will be burned. He will never see them. We will not be shamed before the masses, as religion has supposed. They will simply be destroyed.

The final judgment is the Great White Throne Judgment. (Revelation 20:11-15) In this judgment, those who have rejected the free gift of righteousness in Jesus will, by their own choosing, stand before God, seeking to be declared righteous by their works. They refuse to be judged by Jesus' work.

As we know, by the works of the flesh, no one will be justified before God. This blatant act of arrogant self-righteousness vindicates God's justice before all of creation.

> *Then I saw a great white throne and Him who sat on it, from whose face the earth and the heaven fled away. And there was found no place for them. 12 And I saw the dead, small and great, standing before God, and books were opened. And another book was opened, which is the Book of Life. And the dead were judged according to their works, by the things which were written in the books. 13 The sea gave up the dead who were in it, and Death and Hades delivered up the dead who were in them. And they were judged, each one according to his works. 14 Then Death and Hades were cast into the lake of fire. This is the second death. 15 And anyone not found written in the Book of Life was cast into the lake of fire.* (Revelation 20:11-15 NKJV)

The eternal outcome of the wicked is not God's choice; it is theirs. They love their wickedness, and after 1000 years of Jesus ruling on earth and modeling a perfect world under his rule, they still want a wicked world where they can gratify the lusts of their flesh. They hate righteousness.

In fact, they hate righteousness so much that after Jesus proves to them that the world could have been heaven on earth, they will still gather together for one last attempt to overthrow God and regain their unrighteous control over planet Earth.

The wicked don't want God, and they don't want righteousness. If they were able to abide with the righteous, there would be a repeat of what happened on planet Earth; there would never be eternal righteousness, peace, and joy!

22. Judgment Future

Finally, we are at the sixth and final "Foundation of Faith." I trust that your relationship with God has been ignited through this book. As you invest in your heart and change your belief system, you will begin to see long-term results, which will provide a consistent and stable relationship with God.

For many Christians, their relationship with God is anything but consistent. It is a series of ups and downs, highs and lows, or mountains and valleys. That is not the way things should be when you understand the true nature and character of God. When you understand the finished work of the Cross, your Christian life should become stable.

During this final New Covenant foundational teaching, we will be dealing with a topic that has tremendous potential to transform your life. The majority of Christians that I have met live their lives with a fear of God's judgment. They live with a dread of that day when they will stand before God and be judged. The truth is, if you are in Christ and have been born-again, you are the righteousness of God because of Christ's sacrifice. You don't need to fear the future judgment.

As we look at the teaching of the doctrine of eternal judgment, open your heart and allow the Holy Spirit to teach you. This might be completely contrary to what you've been taught about judgment in the past. I would encourage you to explore this and see if what I am saying is scripturally correct. Judgment for you as a believer is in the past. You have already been judged. You were judged righteous when you put your faith in Jesus

Christ. Therefore, the judgment that you have to look forward to is one of rewards. It is a time and place of receiving a thank-you for the things that you did in this life. There will be a day of judgment for every person in this world- believers and unbelievers. As a believer, we don't need to fear God's judgment.

Church History

Since the beginning of church history, there have always been misconceptions about judgment and about the future judgment. No other doctrine has been used by religious leaders as much as this one to create fear and control among the people. The church throughout the Middle Ages used the fear of judgment to control the common, uneducated people. To this day, ministers of the Gospel, pastors, and teachers use the fear of judgment to control and bring people to Jesus. They fail to realize that whatever motive you use to bring a person to Christ is what will be needed to keep them. That is why mercy triumphs over judgment, and God's kindness should lead us to repentance.

Because of these abuses, many people switch to another extreme. Martin Luther said it best when he said, *"Doctrine is like a drunk man riding a horse. He falls off one side of the horse, gets back up, then falls off the other side of the horse."* We have trouble maintaining the middle ground of truth and embracing the paradoxes found in scripture.

What we are seeing take place currently, especially among believers that emphasize grace and the finished work of the Cross, is a tendency to deny this fundamental doctrine about the judgment to come. All around the world, we are seeing the growth of a movement of Christian Universalism. If you're not familiar with that terminology, this is a doctrine that says that "in the end, everyone will be saved." Therefore, there will not be a future judgment or a literal hell because the whole world will be saved. That sounds good, and we do know that God is not willing that any would perish, but that all would come to repentance, but Universalism is clearly not what scripture teaches.

There is another doctrine called Trinitarian Theology or Inclusionism. This doctrine, much like Christian Universalism, teaches that because

Jesus died for everyone and included the whole world in his death on the Cross, he, therefore, included everyone in the resurrection, producing salvation. It proclaims that the whole world has already been saved and born-again, and therefore there is no need for personal faith in Jesus. The outcome is the same, denial of the judgment to come and denial of a literal hell. Inclusionism says that everyone has already been saved, and Universalism says that the whole world will be saved.

The Bible very clearly teaches that every one of us will stand before God. It is appointed for man to die once and after that to face the judgment. As a believer, you don't need to fear judgment because it's not going to be the way that you were probably taught. But we have to understand that as we emphasize God's grace, mercy, and goodness, they are never at the expense of God's justice. God is kind because he is good, but he ultimately will punish evil.

> **THE BIBLE VERY CLEARLY TEACHES THAT EVERY ONE OF US WILL STAND BEFORE GOD. IT IS APPOINTED FOR MAN TO DIE ONCE AND AFTER THAT TO FACE THE JUDGMENT.**

The Great White Throne Judgment

The Bible talks about two judgments. There is the Great White Throne Judgment, described in Revelation chapter 20, and there is the judgment seat of Christ. Many mix the two together, but these are two unique and separate judgments. One is for believers, and one is for unbelievers. Let's look first at the Great White Throne Judgment. You do not want to be present for this one, and I have good news for you, if you are born-again, you will not be there.

> *Then I saw a great white throne and Him who sat on it, from whose face the earth and the heaven fled away. And there was found no place for them. [12] And I saw the dead, small and great, standing before God, and books were opened. And another book was opened, which is the Book of Life. And the dead were judged according to their works, by the things which were written in the books. [13] The sea*

gave up the dead who were in it, and Death and Hades delivered up the dead who were in them. And they were judged, each one according to his works. ^{14} Then Death and Hades were cast into the lake of fire. This is the second death. ^{15} And anyone not found written in the Book of Life was cast into the lake of fire. (Revelation 20:11-15 NKJV)

We need to ask, "What is the Book of Life, and whose names are written in it?" Other places in scripture teach us that the Book of Life is where the names of all who believe in Jesus Christ are recorded. Therefore, if your name is not written in the Book of Life, you will be one of those who stand before the Great White Throne Judgment. Those who have never received grace as a gift and the righteousness of God will be judged according to their works. Why? Because they rejected the gift of righteousness. In essence, they said, judge me according to my righteousness.

The judgment at the Great White Throne is not for believers. This is for people who reject the gift of righteousness and want to be judged according to their works. Acts 17:31 NKJV says, *"He has appointed a day on which he will judge the world in righteousness by the man whom he has ordained. He has given assurances of this to all by raising him from the dead."*

God, through Jesus, will judge the world in righteousness. His judgment will be entirely just and truthful, and none will be punished because of individual acts of sin. Judgment is based on one sin, the sin of unbelief in Jesus.

"And when He has come, He will convict the world of sin, and of righteousness, and of judgment: of sin, because they do not believe in Me..." (John 16:8-9 NKJV)

Jesus said he would send the Holy Spirit, who will convict the world of sin, righteousness, and of judgment. Then he says, "Of sin, because they don't believe in me." He is saying that the Holy Spirit has not come to point out every individual act of sin. He doesn't come to show the world what's wrong with them. The Holy Spirit comes to convince the world that they need a Savior, to convict of unbelief.

Therefore, this judgment will be based on how people responded to the Gospel. Did they receive or reject the gift of righteousness through faith alone? Rejection of faith-righteousness will condemn us. It's not God condemning us; it's the rejection of the payment for our sins.

John 5:22 NKJV says, *"For the Father judges no one, but has committed all judgment to the son."*

John 12:47- 48 NIV says:

> *And if anyone hears my words but does not keep them, I do not judge that person For I did not come to judge the world, but to save the world. There is a judge for the one who rejects me and does not accept my word; the very words I have spoken will condemn them at the last day.*

This judgment will be according to the Gospel, and the judgment at the Great White Throne will be based on what we did with the message of Jesus Christ. To reject grace is to choose by default to be punished according to our works, as no flesh can stand in the presence of God.

Chapter Questions

1. Why is the doctrine of eternal judgment essential?

2. What are some of the deceptions that come when people deny eternal judgment?

3. Has what you have been taught about this subject made you fearful about judgment? If so, why?

23. Judgment Past

As a believer, you will not stand before the Great White Throne Judgment. You have already been judged as righteous. The judgment for your sin is past.

Let's look in John:

> *Now is the judgment of this world; now the ruler of this world will be cast out.* [32] *And I, if I am lifted up from the earth, will draw all peoples to Myself."* [33] *This He said, signifying by what death He would die.* (John 12:31-33 NKJV)

When does John say the judgment is going to take place? Now! Jesus said this over 2000 years ago. He said, *"Now is the judgment of this world."* He was going to the Cross. He was declaring that judgment was about to take place. Then he said, *"Now the ruler of this world* (the devil) *will be cast out."* Jesus defeated the devil by his death, burial, and resurrection over 2000 years ago. Jesus continues, *"And if I am lifted up from the earth, I will draw all people to myself."*

In your Bible, depending upon the translation you use, some of you will see that the word "peoples" is in italics. If there's a word in italics, it shows that the word is not in the original manuscripts, as the translators added it for clarity.

What Jesus actually said is, *"If I am lifted up from the earth, I will draw all to myself."* Translators inserted the word "peoples" because it seemed to them to make sense. The only issue is that not everyone has been drawn to Jesus. Though he is available for everyone, not everyone has come to Jesus. There is a different way of looking at that scripture. Remember, the context is judgment. I believe that what Jesus is saying here, and many theologians will agree, is that through the Cross, Jesus drew, not all people, but all judgment to himself. All of God's righteous judgment toward sin was placed on Jesus, and Jesus was judged. He took all judgment for sin, and this happened over 2000 years ago, long before you were ever born or had done anything good or bad.

Jesus our propitiation

> PROPITIATION MEANS THE "SATISFYING OF JUDGMENT OR WRATH."

There is a theological word used in scripture called "propitiation." Propitiation means the "satisfying of judgment or wrath." The Bible uses it in reference to Jesus, who satisfied in his body all the righteous judgment that God has toward sin. He satisfied it in his own body on the Cross. God is not angry or filled with wrath. He's not angry at people, but he is a righteous judge. Now because He is righteous, he has wrath against sin. We all know that God has wrath against sin, but most people don't understand how God dealt with sin without destroying the human race.

My friends, this is the doctrine of propitiation. Jesus actually became our sin and took the consequences and punishment for the sins of all people. He died the death that we deserved.

Every year on the Day of Atonement, under the Old Covenant (Leviticus 16), the Israelites would take their sacrifices to the door of the Tent of Meeting. Then the priests would take two goats. The first was a sin offering for the sins of the people. The goats had to be pure; they had to be spotless. The priest would lay hands on the first goat and confess the sins of the people over the goat. Then the goat was sacrificed, its blood was drained, and it was judged in place of the worshippers. The sacrificed goat represents propitiation. This signified that the wrath and the judgment of God, for that year, was turned aside and placed on that goat, and that it was dying in place of the people.

Next, the priest would place his hands on the head of the second goat, called the scapegoat, and transfer the sins of the people to the head of that goat. This goat represents expiation, where the goat bore Israel's sins, which were then sent away and removed. This speaks of when Jesus Christ went to the Cross, and all sin was placed on Jesus. God, in essence, confessed those sins over Jesus so that we could go free. The second goat was not killed but was released into the wilderness, where it would bear the sins of the people. That is what Jesus Christ did for us. Not only did he die like the first goat as a sacrifice, but as the second goat, he sent away and removed our sins and bore our sins to hell, and he left them there so that we could be absolutely free of the fear of judgment. This sacrifice by Jesus, unlike the temporary sacrifices on the Day of Atonement, did not have to be done yearly but was once and for all time! (Hebrews 9)

> *My little children, these things I write to you, so that you may not sin. And if anyone sins, we have an Advocate with the Father, Jesus Christ the righteous. ² And He Himself is the propitiation for our sins, and not for ours only but also for the whole world.* (1 John 2:1-2 NKJV)

Jesus is the propitiation. He is the one that stands in our place and takes away the wrath of God for our sins. This is not only for ours but also for the sins of the whole world. It is very clear that Jesus died not only for our sins but for the sins of the world. He satisfied the righteous judgment for the sins of all, believers and unbelievers.

Therefore, sin is not the main issue separating people from God. The big question is, will you receive the forgiveness provided for you? Sin has been paid for; it has been dealt with. When did Jesus become our propitiation? When did he take away our sins? It was on the Cross. It was before you, and I were born that Jesus dealt with the sin problem. Our sin was judged before we ever committed any sin. The judgment for sins is past; Jesus was judged in our place. Jesus paid the price so all people could come to God. But now we have a choice whether we will accept this by faith.

Be reconciled to God

> *Now all things are of God, who has reconciled us to Himself through Jesus Christ, and has given us the ministry of reconciliation, ^{that} is,*

> *that God was in Christ reconciling the world to Himself, not imputing their trespasses to them, and has committed to us the word of reconciliation.* (2 Corinthians 5:18-19 NKJV)

From God's standpoint, the sins of the world have been judged and dealt with. Yet we must receive this through faith and be born-again and transformed. That is why he goes on and speaks:

> *Now then, we are ambassadors for Christ, as though God were pleading through us: we implore you on Christ's behalf, be reconciled to God. [21] For He made Him who knew no sin to be sin for us, that we might become the righteousness of God in Him.* (2 Corinthians 5:20-21 NKJV)

The world is not automatically saved, even though God is not holding the sins of the world against it, even though sin has been judged, and even though God has reconciled himself through the body of Jesus to the world. The world, in the form of each person, must personally receive that reconciliation by putting faith in what Jesus accomplished. Marriage takes two. Yes, God gave first through the death, burial, and resurrection of Jesus. He is now waiting for our "Yes!"

> *"Most assuredly, I say to you, he who hears My word and believes in Him who sent Me has everlasting life, and shall not come into judgment, but has passed from death into life."* (John 5:24 NKJV)

Can it get any clearer than that? He who believes in Jesus has eternal life. If you believe in him, you possess eternal life right now and will not come into judgment. This is stated in the past tense- you have already passed from death into life. Understanding that you have already been judged righteous will remove the fear and dread of judgment from your life.

Chapter Questions

1. Why and how did Jesus draw all judgment to himself? What does that mean for you?

2. With this understanding, how should you now live your life?

3. What will free you from all fear of judgment?

24. The Judgment Seat of Christ

What about believers? Where will we stand for the judgment? If we are not going to stand before the Great White Throne Judgment, where will we be?

The Bible talks about the (Bema) judgment seat of Christ. This is a different Greek word and concept from what is used to describe the Great White Throne Judgment that we previously discussed. The idea of the (Bema) judgment seat of Christ takes the reader back to the Greek Olympic times. The (Bema) judgment seat was that place where you received rewards for what you did in the Olympic games. What the Apostle Paul was trying to communicate is that we are not going to stand before God to be judged and critiqued on what we did and didn't do in this life. Instead, we will have the opportunity to stand before God and receive rewards based on how faithful we were to what tasks God put in our hands.

> *Therefore, we make it our aim, whether present or absent, to be well pleasing to Him. For we must all appear before the judgment seat of Christ, that each one may receive the things done in the body, according to what he has done, whether good or bad.* (2 Corinthians 5:9-10 NKJV)

The Bema seat was a place at the Greek games for rendering a verdict or passing a sentence, either in your favor or not. It was a place of rewards, depending on how well you ran your race.

In this third section, we have discussed the foundational doctrine of repentance from dead works. We discussed how every one of us has a list of those things that we try to do to earn favor, earn right standing, and earn the promises of God. Under the new and better covenant, we're called to repent of those dead works and to put faith in God through what Jesus did.

We considered how dead works and good works can look the same and oftentimes are identical; what separates them is our heart motivation. When we stand before God at the judgment seat of Christ, we will give an account of our lives, which will reveal what was done from a heart of love versus what was done from a heart of guilt, obligation, fear, or performance.

We will be rewarded for the good works that we did in response to what God has done for us through Jesus Christ. This is what the Apostle Paul was emphasizing in 1 Corinthians 3:11-16 NKJV. He begins by saying:

> *For no other foundation can anyone lay than that which is laid, which is Jesus Christ."*
>
> *Now if anyone builds on this foundation with gold, silver, precious stones, wood, hay, straw, each one's work will become clear; for the Day will declare it, because it will be revealed by fire; and the fire will test each one's work, of what sort it is. If anyone's work which he has built on it endures, he will receive a reward. If anyone's work is burned, he will suffer loss; but he himself will be saved, yet so as through fire. Do you not know that you are the temple of God and that the Spirit of God dwells in you?*

All believers will stand before the judgment seat of Christ. The day of judgment for believers is going to reveal the quality that we used in building on the foundation of Jesus Christ, be it gold, silver, precious stones, wood, hay, or straw. Our works will be revealed and tested by fire. The fire of God will test the quality of each person's work.

Good news!

This is good news! Imagine yourself coming before the judgment seat of Christ holding on to all those things that you did, things which you think are monumental. But the truth is, our works done with the wrong motivation are dung and trash. Imagine that you are holding onto these works, thinking you will impress God by what you have accomplished. The truth is, they are dead works, and they smell rotten because they're done out of self-righteousness.

What Paul is trying to help us understand is that our works are going to be tested by fire. Imagine that you are walking up to God, carrying all these works that you are trusting in to earn right standing with God. Then the fire of God comes down and burns them all up. The only thing you are left with is what you will be rewarded for, the good works you did as a response to grace, with a heart of gratitude and love.

> **THE ONLY THING YOU ARE LEFT WITH IS WHAT YOU WILL BE REWARDED FOR, THE GOOD WORKS YOU DID AS A RESPONSE TO GRACE, WITH A HEART OF GRATITUDE AND LOVE.**

Truly that should be all that we really desire to have when we stand before God. We don't want our dead works. We don't want our self-righteousness. We don't want all the works that we did trying to move or impress God. We just want the good works done in response to God's grace and love. Therefore, when Paul talks about the fire revealing the quality of our works, that is an act of God's mercy because the rewards are based on what we did out of love rather than obligation or performance.

"For we are His workmanship, created in Christ Jesus for good works, which God prepared beforehand that we should walk in them." (Ephesians 2:10 NKJV)

In Christ, we have been recreated to live a life of good works, but those good works are a response to grace, not what we try to do to impress or move God.

He says, *"If anyone's work is burned, he will suffer loss, but he himself will be saved yet as through fire."* Understand, your salvation is secure. If you have been born-again, you do not need to fear or be afraid of the judgment seat of Christ. However, we also need to understand that the only thing we can bring with us is what we have done for God in response to grace. I don't know about you, but I don't want to stand before God empty-handed, lacking good works.

I long to have something to show for my life. I desire to have a trail of good works following me. I think of the thousands of people that have come to know Jesus Christ through our ministry and our home for orphans in Africa. There will be rewards based on what we accomplished with what we have been given by God, not only for the big things but also for the small things in our day-to-day life. We will be rewarded for those good works done with a heart of love.

You are his managers

You may remember Jesus telling the story of the talents in Matthew 25:14-30. He explained that the Kingdom of God is like a man who gave his stewards or managers different talents (a sum of money or weight of money) before he went on a trip. To one, he gave ten talents, five talents to another, and to the final one, he gave one. The one with the ten went and invested his master's talents/money/abilities and gained ten more. When the master came, he rewarded him and put him in charge of ten cities. Likewise, the man with five received similar rewards. When the man with one came, he said to the master, *"I was afraid because I saw you as a hard man and so I dug, and I hid your talent."* The master was angry and took the talent away and gave it to the one that had been given the ten talents.

Jesus emphasized the need to be faithful stewards. We ought to invest the gifts that God has given to us because our rewards will be based on what we did with what God invested in our lives. To some degree, what we do for eternity will be based on our faithfulness in this life. Jesus talked about there being cities and major areas of responsibility and influence that these stewards were given to take care of based on their faithfulness and response to his grace. Jesus is not saying it's by your works that you're going to be rewarded, but our rewards are based on our response to what God did for us through Jesus Christ.

I hope this has helped you because, as a believer, you don't need to fear judgment. In Christ, we have already been judged as righteous. Yet at the same time, we need to be very clear that there will be the judgment seat of Christ, and we will be rewarded based on our faithfulness and response to the Gospel.

No fear in love

A proper understanding of this doctrine of eternal judgment will remove the dread so you can live your life free from the fear of judgment. You will live a productive life. I love the way John, the apostle of love, put it.

> *In this [union and communion with Him] love is brought to completion and attains with us, that we may have confidence for the day of judgment [with assurance and boldness to face Him], because as He is, so are we in this world. There is no fear in love [dread does not exist], but full-grown (complete, perfect) love turns fear out of doors and expels every trace of terror! For fear brings with it the thought of punishment, and [so] he who is afraid has not reached the full maturity of love [is not yet grown into love's complete perfection].* (1 John 4:17-18 Amplified Bible)

Fear (terror) of God and the love of God cannot co-exist. There is a biblical and Godly fear or reverence of God, but it is not being afraid of God in the traditional meaning. When the Bible speaks of the fear of God, it refers to an honor and a reverence that produces worship. This is the result of knowing God's true character and nature. Being afraid of God involves torment. If you are living in fear of God, and you fear his judgment, then you are living in torment. Love and fear cannot co-exist. His perfect love will drive fear out. Love will push fear out; it will expel fear. If you have a fear problem, the answer is the love of God, not your love for God, but God's love for you. You need to grasp the personal unconditional love of your Father. The perfect love of God will drive out fear.

His blood speaks

How do we apply this to our lives? We need to ask ourselves if we really believe the message of the Cross. Do we believe it, or do we just intellectualize it? The Bible says that the blood of Jesus speaks a better word. This is in reference to Genesis when Cain killed Abel, and God said that the blood of Abel cried out from the ground. His innocent blood called out for vengeance and judgment. The author of Hebrews says that the blood of Jesus speaks a better word, and this word declares our innocence and righteousness. Do you believe this message?

Secondly, ask yourself if you are spending your life in a way that will positively influence eternity. These are questions for the heart. Are you living your life in such a way that you are setting yourself up for rewards on the day of judgment? We have this short time on earth that is going to determine what we will be doing for eternity. No one can take your eternal rewards from you. And likewise, this is the only investment that has a guaranteed return for all of eternity. Jesus said of this that thieves can't break in and steal, rust can't corrupt, moths can't destroy, and it won't devalue over time. What you do for Jesus Christ in this life and the sacrifices you make are eternal, and they will last forever.

The doctrine of eternal judgment is only bad news if you have rejected Jesus Christ. If that is the case, you will be judged according to your works, and you'll be judged at the Great White Throne Judgment. So, repent! Change your mind about the Lord Jesus Christ and believe the Good News of his finished work on your behalf!

If you have been born-again, you have been judged as righteous. Therefore, when you stand before the Judgment Seat of Christ, you will be rewarded based on what you did with the life that God gave us. Did you serve as a faithful steward and child? This Good News removes the fear of judgment and puts us in a place to make an impact on our world.

Chapter Questions

1. On what will the Judgment to Come be based?
2. What takes place at the Judgment Seat of Christ?
3. What takes place at the Great White Throne Judgment?

Section 9 Experiencing Transformation

25. The Goal of the Gospel

The Bible promises a wonderful quality of life to the person who believes. Nowhere in scripture does it say that God wants his children to struggle until death. Jesus did not tell the steward in Luke 16 to struggle and just get by until he comes, nor to just hang in there until he went to heaven. Jesus told the man to do business. A faithful and wise steward is one who is involved, engaged, and prospering in life.

This may be difficult to accept for those who have grown up in the belief or have been taught to believe that suffering equals godliness or that poverty equates to piety. These medieval doctrines have caused much of the world to be turned off toward the true Gospel. The theology of divine chastisement has been used to control multitudes of sincere believers and keep them in bondage to the fear of God, fear of success, and fear of doing anything truly great. For many, self-abasement is falsely called humility. Pride, however, is when we ignorantly refuse to call ourselves what God calls us and to be who God has made us to be in Christ.

The truths that you have discovered in this book have the potential to become seeds of progress and change. They can propel you out of frustration and failure and into the remarkable quality of life for which God created you and purposely redeemed you to experience.

Abundant living

In John 10:10 NKJV, Jesus makes a statement that still confuses the religious mind. He says,

"I have come that they may have life, and that they may have it more abundantly."

The word abundant means to surpass or exceed until over-flowing. Abundant is the opposite of stingy and just getting by in life. Jesus came to give you an over-the-top, abounding, and excessively good life. The word "life" is the Greek word Zoe, which speaks of the quality of life experienced by the one giving it. Therefore, one of the purposes for which Jesus came was to include us in his abounding quality of life.

Here is the verse, as quoted in some other translations:

"But I have come to give you everything in abundance, more than you expect — life in its fullness until you overflow!" (John 10:10 TPT)

"I came so they can have real and eternal life, more and better life than they ever dreamed of." (John 10:10 The Message)

With that said, let's read the whole verse:

"The thief does not come except to steal, and to kill, and to destroy. I have come that they may have life, and that they may have it more abundantly." (John 10:10 NKJV)

If you are like me, you have always interpreted the thief as the devil- Satan. However, the context has nothing to do with Satan. Now don't get me wrong, the devil is the author of death and destruction, not God! Not ever! God is a good God; he wills only good, and he gives out only life. Sickness, death, poverty, and anything else that steals life, kills dreams, or destroys people's health and hopes have their roots in the Accuser, NOT in our Father God.

However, when you read John 10:10 in context, Jesus is addressing the religious leaders. They were misrepresenting God and building walls to keep people out of the Kingdom. They should have instead been building bridges so that people could come to God and experience an amazing and fulfilling life. This is made clear in the following scriptures:

> *Then some of the Pharisees who were with Him heard these words, and said to Him, "Are we blind also?" Jesus said to them, "If you were blind, you would have no sin; but now you say, 'We see.' Therefore, your sin remains.' (John 9:40-41 NKJV)*

> *"Most assuredly, I say to you, he who does not enter the sheepfold by the door, but climbs up some other way, the same is a thief and a robber...".* (John 10:1 NKJV)

> *Then Jesus said to them again, "Most assuredly, I say to you, I am the door of the sheep. All who ever came before Me are thieves and robbers, but the sheep did not hear them. I am the door. If anyone enters by Me, he will be saved, and will go in and out and find pasture. The thief does not come except to steal, and to kill, and to destroy. I have come that they may have life, and that they may have it more abundantly.* (John 10:7-10 NKJV)

Religion today, just as in Jesus' day, steals, kills, and destroys the abundant life that Jesus came to give you. Jesus, in rebuking the religious leaders of the day, called them thieves and robbers. They were attempting to access the Kingdom illegally through their own efforts or works instead of entering through Jesus, the true Door. These religious leaders misrepresented God and used God's good law as a system to keep people in bondage instead of bringing them into freedom.

The Bible is full of outstanding promises. It has promises of health and healing, promises of success and prosperity, and promises of peace and security. As a believer, we read these promises and attempt to attain their fulfillment in our lives. But like the religious Jews of Jesus' day, we attach our religious ideas to the promises. We pursue their fulfillment as a wage to be earned instead of a promise to be received. Preachers tell us that faith is the key and that we must try harder to believe God. We examine our faith (or lack thereof) and retreat back into the shadows of mediocrity and defeat. Friends, I have good news for you! The abundant life that you have desired is not only God's will for you, but it is already within your grasp. In this short book, you will begin to discover real biblical faith. You will have begun to tap into the life of Christ and a quality of living that Jesus called "easy and light."

Chapter Questions

1. How have religious traditions robbed you of abundant living?

2. Label a few of the false beliefs that you have held onto, and then replace them with the truth.

3. Write a few of the promises from the Bible that you desire to see fulfilled in your life.

26. Heaven on Earth

One morning, while I was reading my Bible, I stumbled across this verse:

"That your days may be multiplied, and the days of your children, in the land which the Lord swore unto your fathers to give them, as the days of heaven upon the earth." (Deuteronomy 11:21 KJV)

I began to reflect on what this verse might mean. I decided to research it in the Hebrew since many of the modern translations express it by saying *"as the days of the heavens above the earth."* Sure enough, the original language was crystal clear. God was inviting his chosen people into a promise and a realm where they could experience heaven on earth.

God was making this unbelievable promise to the children of Israel as they prepared to enter into the Promised Land. Moses knew his time had ended; Joshua was being commissioned to lead. On those plains of Moab, the Prophet Moses gave his last address to the children of Israel, whom he had led out of Egypt.

To several million people, Moses exhorted them to follow God's prescribed way, to stay faithful, to love him, and to serve him.

> *For if you carefully keep all these commandments which I command you to do—to love the Lord your God, to walk in all His ways, and to hold fast to Him— then the Lord will drive out all these nations from before you, and you will dispossess greater and mightier nations than yourselves. Every place on which the sole of your foot treads shall be yours.* (Deuteronomy 11:22-24 NKJV)

The result would be that God would lead his people into the good land. Every need would be provided; it would be a slice of heaven upon the earth. Listen to the way Deuteronomy puts it:

> *For the LORD your God is bringing you into a good land, a land of brooks of water, of fountains and springs, that flow out of valleys and hills; a land of wheat and barley, of vines and fig trees and pomegranates, a land of olive oil and honey; a land in which you will eat bread without scarcity, in which you will lack nothing; a land whose stones are iron and out of whose hills you can dig copper. When you have eaten and are full, then you shall bless the LORD your God for the good land which He has given you.* (Deuteronomy 8:7-10 NKJV)

It is important to understand that for the Hebrew listener, heaven on earth was the equivalent of the Garden of Eden. When God gave them the promise that if they obeyed his voice, it would be heaven on earth for them, the Hebrew man or woman's mind would shift back to Eden, the garden of God. They would recall the stories their parents had told them of a time when everything was well on planet Earth, before sin entered in, bringing with it the death and destruction that now plagues the earth and humanity. They remembered when God walked and talked with the man and the woman, and they enjoyed nearness with their Creator. At that time, they were happy, and their bodies were strong; they did not get old, they did not get sick, and they did not die. God himself provided for them; they had abundance in every way.

> **ONLY BY SEEING THE BLUEPRINT CAN WE UNDERSTAND THE PROCESS AND PROPERLY DETERMINE THE GOAL THAT GOD HAS IN MIND.**

To properly understand the heart of God for Heaven on earth and a return to Eden, we must take a trip back to the beginning and start from ground zero. Only by seeing the blueprint can we understand the process and properly determine the goal that God has in mind. Genesis chapters 1-3 should become the foundation for understanding the abundant life God created us to experience. Allow me to take the time to go back and lay a bit of a foundation for the rest of the story.

> *Then God said, "Let Us make man in Our image, according to Our likeness; let them have dominion over the fish of the sea, over the birds of the air, and over the cattle, over all the earth and over every creeping thing that creeps on the earth." So, God created man in His own image; in the image of God, He created him; male and female He created them. Then God blessed them, and God said to them, "Be fruitful and multiply; fill the earth and subdue it; have dominion over the fish of the sea, over the birds of the air, and over every living thing that moves on the earth.* (Genesis 1:26-28 NKJV)

God declares the dignity and equality of all people. The Bible says that we are made in the image of God. Psalms 8:5 says we have been "crowned with glory and honor," which also could be translated as dignity and worth. People are made with intricate value and are made in the image and likeness of our Creator, God, and Father. God did not create one person to be over another or one color or culture to dominate another. He created each individual unique. These verses speak of equality. Both man and woman are created in the image of God. Men were not created to dominate or control women. Both male and female represent God's nature and character. These verses also speak of our purpose and God-given authority on earth. God said we have been given dominion over the world; he said to be fruitful and to multiply.

"The heaven, even the heavens, are the LORD's; But the earth He has given to the children of men." (Psalms 115:16 NKJV)

We were created to steward this earth for the glory of God. As we faithfully take care of the earth, the earth itself brings forth abundance and prosperity. All this and more would come forth from following God's way.

A relationship of love and trust

God created people for a relationship built on love and trust. Love must always give choices. Love that is forced is not love; it is abuse. God created man and woman with the power to love, and at the same time, the opportunity existed to reject his love. Love is risky, and God took a risk in creating people. He did this because he loved us and desired a real relationship. Love must always provide freedom, and freedom is always a risk and potential liability to the one who gives it. God saw you and me as being worth taking a chance. God told Adam and Eve to trust his word. Out of loving obedience, they were to be responsible for and to care for God's beautiful creation. Out of this place of secure relationship, Adam and Eve could fulfill their purpose and, at the same time, live in God's peace, favor, provision, and wholeness.

The Garden of Eden became God's blueprint for redemption. The quality of life that Adam and Eve enjoyed in the garden was and still is God's desire for mankind. Jesus came as the ransom. His sacrifice on the Cross was the payment to restore to us all that Adam and Eve had lost. Clearly, this is more than just forgiveness and a ticket to heaven. Redemption provides and restores back to us everything that was lost through Adam's rebellion. This is the goal of the Gospel, a relationship of love and trust with our Creator Father that places us in a place to experience everything provided for us in Christ Jesus.

Chapter Questions

1. What would heaven on earth mean for you?
2. What needs to change in your life in order to experience God's best for you?

27. Conditioning Your Heart

If you are reading this book, you have a desire to experience the transforming power of God in your life. In Mark chapter 4, Jesus gave what we call the parable of the sower. Though familiar to most, I would say very few believers truly grasp the significance of this parable. In fact, Jesus asked his disciples in Mark 4:13 NKJV, *"Do you not understand this parable? How then will you understand all the parables?"*

Jesus was giving his disciples the key to understanding how his Word works in their lives. In a sense, this is the Rosetta Stone of unlocking the power of the Word of God and its ability to work in your life.

This is what he said:

> *Listen! Behold, a sower went out to sow. ⁴ And it happened, as he sowed, that some seed fell by the wayside; and the birds of the air came and devoured it. ⁵ Some fell on stony ground, where it did not have much earth; and immediately it sprang up because it had no depth of earth ⁶ But when the sun was up it was scorched, and because it had no root it withered away.⁷ And some seed fell among thorns; and the thorns grew up and choked it, and it yielded no crop. ⁸ But other seed fell on good ground and yielded a crop that sprang up, increased and produced: some thirtyfold, some sixty, and some a hundred." ⁹ And He said to them, "He who has ears to hear, let him hear!"* (Mark 4:3-8 NKJV)

He went on to give the explanation to his disciples, those who have ears to hear.

> *And He said to them, "Do you not understand this parable? How then will you understand all the parables? ¹⁴ The sower sows the word. ¹⁵ And these are the ones by the wayside where the word is sown. When they hear, Satan comes immediately and takes away the word that was sown in their hearts. ¹⁶ These likewise are the ones sown on stony ground who, when they hear the word, immediately receive it with gladness; ¹⁷ and they have no root in themselves, and so endure only for a time. Afterward, when tribulation or persecution arises for the word's sake, immediately they stumble. ¹⁸ Now these are the ones sown among thorns; they are the ones who hear the word, ¹⁹ and the cares of this world, the deceitfulness of riches, and the desires for other things entering in choke the word, and it becomes unfruitful. ²⁰ But these are the ones sown on good ground, those who hear the word, accept it, and bear fruit: some thirtyfold, some sixty, and some a hundred.* (Mark 4:3-9,13-20 NKJV)

We need to understand that the ground to which Jesus is referring, where the seed of his Word is sown, is the ground of our heart. Therefore, it is the condition of our heart which determines if and how the Word will work in our life. Throughout this book, you have received new ideas and a fresh perspective of God's goodness and the finished work of the Cross. The goal is not just to accumulate information. Paul said in 1 Corinthians 8:1 NKJV, *"Knowledge puffs up, but love builds up."* The goal is that the ground of your heart would be good ground that receives the Word of God, the Word of the New Covenant, and brings forth good fruit.

Next, it is intended that you understand that only you can determine what you will allow into your heart. I'm not saying that you can always control what life brings you or that what you go through in life is your fault. But as you will see, it is the value that you place on those things and the thoughts and meditation you give them that will determine if they enter the ground of your heart or not.

Jesus said it like this:

> *Then He said to them, "Take heed what you hear. With the same measure you use, it will be measured to you; and to you who hear, more will be given. ²⁵ For whoever has, to him more will be given; but whoever does not have, even what he has will be taken away from him.* (Mark 4:24-25 NKJV)

Listen to this verse in the Amplified

And He said to them, "Be careful what you are hearing. The measure [of thought and study] you give [to [l]the truth you hear] will be the measure [l][of virtue and knowledge] that comes back to you—and more [besides] will be given to you who hear."

We are to guard what we hear. What is the message you are allowing into your heart? Is it the Good News of the Gospel, the finished work of the Cross, or is it man's traditions?

Ask yourself these questions:

- Does what you are hearing produce fear or peace?
- Does it create distrust in God and his goodness, or does it develop steadfast trust?
- Does the Gospel that you are hearing create the need to earn what has already been freely given you or a confidence that our inheritance is given freely in Christ?

It is absolutely essential that we guard what we are allowing to come through our ears into our hearts. It will either produce death or life in our relationship with God. *"Cease, my son, to hear the instruction that causeth you to err from the words of knowledge."* (Proverbs 19:27 KJV) We need to cease to listen to any opposing voices, even if they are coming from a so-called man of God. Our heart and relationship with God are much too important!

Not only are we to guard what we are hearing, we are to take heed to how we hear: *"Therefore take heed how you hear."* (Luke 8:18 NKJV) The effect of the Word of the Gospel on our hearts is directly related to what we hear and how we hear it. Do we have ears to hear? Are we teachable? Do we have a repentant attitude? When what we believe is confronted by the truth of the Word of God, do we repent/change our minds, or do we stubbornly protect our ego through unbelief?

Jesus said the degree to that you hear or refuse to hear, you will receive back more. This is not God's judgment but the power of sowing and reaping.

Lastly, this parable tells us that the condition of our hearts is determined and influenced by outside sources and how we respond. Jesus said outside sources, such as persecution, worries of life, and personal desires, can choke out the Word's influence upon our hearts.

Solomon said, *"Keep your heart with all diligence, for out of it spring the issues of life."* (Proverbs 4:23 NKJV) One of the Hebrew definitions for issues is the English word "boundaries." We could say that we must guard our hearts diligently because the condition of our hearts determines our life's boundaries or limitations. We will never rise above or go beyond what we believe in our hearts. There are many sources of limiting beliefs that set the boundaries in our lives. A few obvious ones are listed below:

- Traditions
- Legalism
- Fear
- Unbelief
- Self-image
- Self-worth

Our heart is much too important to allow it to be affected by sin, lies about ourselves or God, or the shallowness of religion. The seed of the Good News, regardless of how small and insignificant it may seem, has the potential to transform your life when received into a good heart. Make the decision now to be the gatekeeper of your heart. Ask yourself if you are allowing anything to enter in that should not be there. Likewise, what do you want to experience that Jesus paid the price to provide for you? In this next chapter, we will discover some of the essential tools for experiencing personal transformation.

Chapter Questions

1. Only you can minister to your heart and determine the influence circumstances have upon it. What have you allowed into your heart that should not be there? Also, what should you be allowing in that you are not?

2. Make a list of the things that Jesus provided that you are not yet experiencing in your life. What steps will you take to persuade your heart to their reality in your life?

28. Putting on the New

Right believing always produces right living, not vice versa. The truths of the Gospel that you have received in this book have the potential to radically transform your life. However, true transformation always works at a heart level and takes place gradually and effortlessly as it works its way from our heart to the outside.

The Apostle Paul laid out the pathway to transformation when he wrote:

> *That you put off, concerning your former conduct, the old man which grows corrupt according to the deceitful lusts, [23] and be renewed in the spirit of your mind, [24] and that you put on the new man which was created according to God, in true righteousness in true righteousness and holiness.* (Ephesians 4:22-24 NKJV)

We are told to put off the old and, through the renewing of our minds, put on the new you, which is already perfectly righteous and holy through Jesus' exchange. Christian maturity is not you working hard to become something that you are not. It is simply you living out of the reality of who you are and what you have through your union with Jesus Christ. This is accomplished as we put off the old and put on the new through a process of renewing our minds and changing the beliefs of our hearts.

Strongholds in our minds

Recently I came across this statistic: the average person has 70,000 thoughts come through their mind every single day. Out of those 70,000 thoughts, for most people, 75% of them are negative. Think about that, 57,000 negative thoughts violating your mind, influencing your beliefs, and poisoning your perspective - every day. King Solomon was onto something when he wrote, *"As he (a man) thinks in his heart so is he."* (Proverbs 23:7 NKJV)

These negative mindsets become something that Paul in 2 Corinthians 10 called a "stronghold" of beliefs. The longer we hold onto them, and the more we think upon them, the more permanent they become. We falsely assume that the battle is with the devil when in fact, our struggle is between our minds and hearts.

That is what Paul called a stronghold.

> *For the weapons of our warfare are not carnal but mighty in God for pulling down strongholds, [5] casting down arguments and every high thing that exalts itself against the knowledge of God, bringing every thought into captivity to the obedience of Christ.* (2 Corinthians 10:4-5 NKJV)

Every time you are confronted with a situation, emotion, or belief other than the reality of what Jesus accomplished for you, there are two questions that you need to ask yourself. First, did Jesus overcome my problem? Secondly, am I "in Christ." If you answered yes to both of those questions, then you already have the answer for which you are looking.

Renewing the mind

Romans 12:2 NKJV says that we are to *"be transformed by the renewing of our minds."* How do we renew or renovate our minds? Jesus gave us the answer:

> *And He said to them, 'Be careful what you are hearing. The measure [of thought and study] you give [to the truth you hear] will be the measure [of virtue and knowledge] that comes back to you—and more [besides] will be given to you who hear."* (Mark 4:24-25 Amplified)

Meditation is the key to transformation. Unlike the New Age concept of meditation, where the focus is the emptying of your mind, the scriptural concept of meditation is to think, ponder, and dwell on a particular scriptural truth until it stirs your imagination and emotions. This is also the scriptural way to write the truth of God's Word upon your heart and, at the same time, renew or rewire your mind.

Scripture, as well as science, tells us that our hearts are influenced through a combination of truth and emotion. When the truth of God's Word is combined with our imagination and emotion (response to God and his Word), the biblical process of transformation begins to take place as we create new beliefs at a heart level.

This may sound strange, but this was the method that God told the children of Israel to employ to be prosperous and successful.

> *This Book of the Law shall not depart from your mouth, but you shall meditate in it day and night, that you may observe to do according to all that is written in it. For then you will make your way prosperous, and then you will have good success.* (Joshua 1:8 NKJV)

The Word was to be in their mouths and in their hearts through meditation. Many people are going around confessing the Word while completely ignoring the fact that what comes out of our mouths must first be believed in our hearts. Yes, our words are vital to influencing our hearts, and I would go so far as to say that you will never go or grow beyond what you are speaking from your mouth. Yet real transformation starts with a persuaded heart, and this is accomplished as we think, study, ponder, and meditate on the truth of the Word of God.

Believe the Good News

Paul told the church in Rome that *"The Gospel is the power of God for the salvation for everyone who believes."* (Romans 1:16 NKJV) As taught earlier in this book, the word 'salvation' ("soteria" in the Greek) is an all-inclusive word that means to save, forgive, heal, deliver, cause to prosper, make whole, and give peace. The Good News believed in the heart is the power of God producing all of these benefits in our lives. Through the finished work of the Cross, you have been made righteous and qualified to participate in the abundant life that God gives.

The investment that you are making in your life as you build a solid foundation on the truths of the New Covenant is absolutely essential for a stable, consistent, and God-honoring life. Already, transformation is taking place, and even now, your mind is being renewed, and you are making the journey. Be blessed.

Chapter Questions

1. Your life is a product of your thoughts and the beliefs of your heart. What thoughts are you allowing into your mind that are not in the mind of God?

2. Transformation is simple- develop a lifestyle of putting off the old man and putting on the new through the renewing of your mind. Consider how this should look in your life on a daily basis.

Conclusion Making the Journey

Dr. Jim Richards

The Foundations of Faith provide a doctrinal basis for righteousness that keeps us from going "off the rails" into legalism or liberalism. According to Scripture, the teaching of God's righteousness is the ultimate stumbling stone. The entire nation of Israel took themselves into self-destruction because they refused to accept God's definition of righteousness. (Romans 9:30-33) How much more should we endeavor to know and experience the righteousness of God, according to Scripture?

The writer of Hebrews pointed out that those believers were still spiritually immature. They were at a place in their lives where they should be teachers of the Word, serving and leading others. Instead, they needed to be "retaught" the very foundations of New Covenant doctrine. (Hebrews 5:12-6:3)

It is the call of every believer to become a disciple, i.e., a person who is building their life on the teachings of the Lord Jesus. And the application of those teachings is to be based on what he modeled in his life! These are not students; they are disciples. Students want to know the information their teacher knows. Disciples want to live the life their teacher lives.

Those who do not respond to the call to be a disciple of the Lord Jesus are like the children of Israel who wandered through the wilderness for forty years, never reaching their destination, never finding a place of rest. They were still God's people, but God could not bring any great degree of benefit to their lives because all they wanted was for him to perform miracles to meet their needs. They showed no interest in learning his ways so they could model his character and goodness to a pagan world.

It should have taken eleven days for Israel to walk from Mount Sinai, where they became a nation, to the land of Canaan, where they would inhabit their nation. Instead, it took forty years, and even then, the people he led out of Egypt that saw all his incredible miracles never entered into his promises. Their children did, however, enter into the promised land! Unlike their parents, they were willing to trust God and follow him. They were disciples!

According to the Apostle Paul, everything that befell them, both good and bad, was recorded so it would be an example for us to understand and thus avoid their failings and follow their examples of that which worked. (1 Corinthians 10:11)

> THE GOAL OF MINISTRY LEADERS IS TO MEND AND EQUIP THE BELIEVER TO SERVE OTHERS IN THE THINGS OF GOD.

According to Ephesians 4:11-16, the goal of ministry leaders is to mend and equip the believer to serve others in the things of God. When that is accomplished, the disciple will be stable and will come into wholeness. They will walk in love, one toward another, and build up the body of Christ.

This is God's goal for every believer. Discipleship is the journey to which we are called! We are called to enter into our inheritance and then serve others in the things of God! When we refuse to pursue those goals, we hamper our own growth and the growth of others. We then become like the children of Israel, having no clear purpose.

The following segments of this book are designed to bring the pieces together into concise, understandable aspects of application. It will not be the fact that you have learned the information in this book that will help you make this journey; it will be because you apply the information to your life!

As you read each segment, determine if you are, in fact, putting these truths into practice!

Living by faith

Martin Luther turned the world upside down based on his revelation from Habakkuk 2:4," *The just shall live by faith."* Somehow, over the last five centuries, this simple statement was twisted into something very different than it says. Let's examine this before attempting to find what this means for us.

The just are those people who are declared righteous by God because they trust Him, i.e., live by faith! But what does that really mean? To a large segment of Christianity, the idea of living by faith is when we believe God to answer our prayers, intervene in our life, and work an occasional miracle.

The Scripture doesn't say God will respond to faith by fulfilling our desires and requests. It doesn't say that if we believe we are righteous, God will grant us righteousness. No! It simply says that if we are righteous, living by faith is the way we are to live. Faith is our approach to life for those who know, trust, and seek to walk with God! This is the way of the disciple!

God is righteous. While righteousness reflects certain character traits, at its core, it simply means "to be right!" God's righteous character is manifested in the fact that he is good and only good. Therefore, all he says and does is for all mankind. However, only those who trust (live by faith) and follow his wisdom participate in the fullness of his goodness.

In the garden, we all know, Adam and Eve ate from the tree of the knowledge of good and evil. Up until that time, they lived by faith. How could they live by faith, you may ask? They were in direct communication with God. That is the rationale of those who think faith is about getting things from God. Adam and Eve trusted God to reveal good and evil to them, and they followed his wisdom!

Faith is not what we do to get God to respond to us. Faith is our response of trust to God. Faith always produces corresponding actions, i.e., behavior! Adam and Eve obeyed God because they trusted him... until they didn't. They were seduced into the idea that if only they could choose good and evil based on their personal opinion, they could live a much more gratifying life. From that point forward, they trusted their opinion more than God's! Their faith was now in themselves instead of God. They trusted themselves more than God! From this, we understand why *it is impossible to please God without faith.* When faith is not present, we are declaring God as untrustworthy and even a liar! We become a god to ourselves.

Good and evil are much more robust concepts in the original language than in English. Good and evil always describe something that is pleasant and desirable as opposed to something unpleasant and undesirable. Good, in Hebrew, always implies harmony. So that which is good maintains our harmony with God; therefore, it keeps us on the pathway of life, light, and blessings. Evil is chaotic and out of harmony with God; therefore, it is a pathway to darkness, death, and destruction.

When man introduced sin, God said he had become flesh. (Genesis 6:3) Whatever else that may have meant, it now implies that mankind defined their life by the degree they could gratify their flesh: lust of the flesh, lust of the eyes, and the pride of life! So, man, as his own god, determined that it was a good thing to live for the gratification of the flesh. While he, no doubt, felt the pleasure of sin for a season, it was a pathway to self-centeredness, greed, self-worship, abuse of his fellowman, and abuse of himself, which always ends in death.

Those who are righteous live by faith; they trust God. They build their lives on God's understanding of good and evil! Faith is more than the belief in the individual promises God has made. Faith is confident in the fact that God is good, He is trustworthy, and he never changes. He never moves from those character traits. They trust what he says because they trust who he is! When there is no trust, producing the intent to follow God, there is no righteousness!

How I read the Scripture

The Bible tells us to seek, and we shall find. This verse also reveals the fact that we will find what we are seeking! In plain language, what I am looking for in Scripture is what I will find, and I will block out that which is contrary to what I am looking for. The Scripture is a testimony of God's interaction with the human race, whereby we can see him as he is and know what to expect from him.

Conclusion Making the Journey

Every believer has their own unique relationship with the Scripture. To the surprise of many, how we relate to the Word of God can make it a life source or a hindrance. It can open our eyes to see God as he is or become the basis for falsely confirming our unscriptural opinions about God, leading us deeper into darkness!

So, the question remains, how can I read Scripture so it becomes a path that leads to Jesus instead of a wall that separates me from him? Jesus said this about how we relate to the Scripture:

"You search the Scriptures, for in them you think you have eternal life; and these are they which testify of Me. But you are not willing to come to Me that you may have life." (John 5:39-40 NKJV)

The Word of God is not our source of life. The word of God is the lamp that makes it possible to see the way to life. Jesus is the life, light, love, and everything we desire for fullness of life.

Do the Scriptures lead me to pursue Jesus personally, or does the information in the Scripture become a substitute for personal intimacy?

When asked how to find eternal life, Jesus responded with these two questions. "*What is written in the Law?' and, 'How do you read it?*" (Luke 10:26 NIV) We often feel that reading the Scripture will always lead us to the answers we need. But studying the Scripture is not what determines how it will affect us. How we read it makes that determination. Why do I read the Scripture? What am I looking for? What is my guiding doctrine? The answers to these questions determine how Scripture will affect us!

Am I a student or a disciple?

Many people inaccurately quote John 8: 32 NKJV to say, "*You shall know the truth, and the truth shall make you free!*" Part of the Scripture does say that, but to lift that part out without the context changes the meaning. He actually presents conditions for the Word to set us free.

Then Jesus said to those Jews who believed him, *"If you abide in My word, you are My disciples indeed. And you shall know the truth, and the truth shall make you free."* (John 8:31-32 NKJV)

First, we must believe in him. Second, we must abide in his Word. Then we should be committed to discipleship. These three bring us to the place to know, i.e., experience his word. Then, because it is experienced, it sets us free. The Word that is not experienced is nothing more than intellectual information.

In John 7:17 NKJV, Jesus says, *"If anyone wills to do His will, he shall know concerning the doctrine, whether it is from God or whether I speak on My own authority."* An expanded translation of this verse would read more like this. "If anyone has the desire or intention to put this into application, he will experientially know whether my doctrine is from God."

The intent to apply God's Word to our lives seems to be the primary factor that determines how we understand it and what we experience. It is only when we experience it that we know it is true. That's when it changes the quality of our life.

Meditative Bible reading

According to Chaim Bentorah, in his book, ***Learning God's Love Language***,[9] the ancient sages had a saying. There are fifty faces to the Torah. There are so many ways to translate the Scripture that we can see several dimensions of application and understanding. The person who studies just to get their doctrine right is probably functioning at the lowest level of Bible study. They usually engage their mind and not their heart, which means the Holy Spirit cannot be our teacher.

I recommend that every time you pray, listen to a sermon, or read the Bible, the cry of your heart should be, "Father, you are my teacher, show me what I need today." This opens our hearts to God as our teacher. After utilizing every tool and research capability, we should take time to reflect on our thoughts and consider, "What did the word say to me today?"

This is not about theology; this is about the application. "Father, based on how I saw this today, what are you saying to me? How will I put this into practice?" I recommend that you jot down a few notes about how to apply this to your life and the steps you will take.

---

9   Chaim Bentorah, Learning the Love Language of God, True Potential

Conclusion Making the Journey

Finally, see and imagine yourself in Christ, putting these things into practice. Experience how the application of this teaching will influence your life. Ponder, consider, and meditate on how you will take these steps. Stay ever aware that Jesus is your Shepherd; trust that he will lead you. Don't jump ahead and attempt to force this into your paradigm.

Seeing God as he is

Contrary to corrupt religious thought, God is very understandable. Obviously, he is beyond our ability to ever fully understand, but everything we need for life and godliness has been revealed. God wants us to understand him.[10] He has gone to great lengths to ensure that we never languish in confusion.

In the occult, the pagan gods are unknowable and unpredictable. They are mysterious; they hold their worshippers in constant fear of making a mistake or incurring their wrath. But God, our Creator and Father, has made Himself known. This is why we must live by faith! The only way we can know God is through what he has revealed. Faith believes what God reveals.

> THE ONLY WAY WE CAN KNOW GOD IS THROUGH WHAT HE HAS REVEALED. FAITH BELIEVES WHAT GOD REVEALS.

Religion would have us believe that faith is blind. God, on the other hand, always wants us to see clearly. Faith is not blind. Faith doesn't shut its eyes, jump off the cliff, and hope there will be a net. Faith is when we believe what God has revealed about himself. And, on that knowledge, we act!

The reason it is impossible to please God apart from faith is based on the fact that God has made all crucial factors clear and simple. Most of what we call a lack of understanding about what to do is actually rooted in unbelief. We just do not believe what God says about himself!

There are myriad ways to see God clearly. Obviously, reading and studying the Bible is the overall way to see and understand God. However, it

10   Dr. Jim Richards, Leadership That Builds People

takes time to study and understand the Bible. And, as previously mentioned, how we read the Bible is the great determining factor about what we get from it. The following six factors help us to be able to understand the Bible when we read it, but more specifically, help us to see and know God as he has chosen to reveal himself.

Jesus' purpose on earth was made clear in everything he did, which glorified God. God is glorified when humans see and acknowledge that he is who he has declared himself to be. Prior to Jesus, no human had ever perceived God as he presented himself. Every belief of every teacher of the Law was tainted with legalistic paganism. It was these teachers, sages, and priests who changed the image of God to their preferences.

God has gone to incredible lengths so people can see him as he is. Therefore, all who refuse to trust God are without excuse! As you will soon see, God has left such a clear witness of himself, no one has an excuse for not knowing and misunderstanding God!

The Bible calls us to be jointly transformed into the likeness of Jesus. This transformation happens in fellowship (communion). Communion, according to the original language, is when two people share that which only belongs to one person.

We, through faith in our hearts, are able to share in every victory Jesus won in the same way, He shared in our every sin and defeat. We become more than conquerors through his victories!

The Scripture provides a clear pathway to absolute victory. It offers specific instructions about how we can influence our hearts to experience the life and power of God. Based on the condition of our hearts, we may fail to see the truth that will establish us in absolute victory.

Creation

Romans 1:20-21says, *"For since the creation of the world His invisible attributes are clearly seen, being understood by the things that are made, even His eternal power and Godhead, so that they are without excuse."*

The first eleven books of Genesis are the beginning of all things relating to God. In these chapters, we have the opportunity to see many of the most important doctrines of the Bible in their first reference. We should all be masters of these first eleven books, but before all things, we must believe the biblical account of creation.

In the physical world, we have the opportunity to see in a physical model truths that became very complex when applied to spiritual and social life. Creation is the first pillar of faith. Those who do not know and believe the biblical account of creation will never be stable in their faith and consistent in their understanding of God.

> THOSE WHO DO NOT KNOW AND BELIEVE THE BIBLICAL ACCOUNT OF CREATION WILL NEVER BE STABLE IN THEIR FAITH AND CONSISTENT IN THEIR UNDERSTANDING OF GOD.

Even among secular researchers and scientists, there is a growing consensus that almost everything we have been told about the history of planet Earth is not only incorrect but is deliberately altered to give influence to those seeking to control the population.

There are a great number of secular scientists that agree that the universe had to be created through intelligent design. Modern-day archeology totally disputes the current model of evolution and the development of human life. The information sciences, which are on the cutting edge of modern research, emphatically oppose the idea that intelligent life can evolve from unintelligent matter.

Discover the truth and teach it to your children while it is still easily found.

The names of God

God provided us with his names to make it abundantly clear who he is and what we should expect from him. The names of God, like names for all mankind, were at one time used to describe certain attributes of the person.

For example, God calls himself by what many refer to as the covenant names of God. In these names, we see clearly how God chooses to relate to His created ones.

Jehovah our righteousness, Jehovah who sanctifies, Jehovah our peace, Jehovah who is present, Jehovah who heals, Jehovah who provides, Jehovah our Shepherd, and Jehovah our banner.

> TO BELIEVE GOD IS DIFFERENT THAN HIS NAMES REVEAL IS TO TAKE THE NAME OF THE LORD OUR GOD IN VAIN.

To believe God is different than his names reveal is to take the name of the Lord our God in vain.

Taking God's name in vain is more than using the word, "God" in conjunction with a curse word. The word for vain in Hebrew is about using the name in a worthless manner. It is appropriate to apply this to using his name in conjunction with any type of profanity

The epitome of taking the name of the Lord in vain may be to identify with his name but then contradict it so as to may it worthless. For example, to believe that Jehovah, who heals, is the one that is making you sick. Or to confess that Jehovah your Shepherd has left you without direction or protection. Most of the bad things for which we blame God are violations of his name, his character, his Covenant, and his Son.

The word confess comes from a compound word that means to "say the same thing," and "logos." To confess the name of Jesus, we must say the same thing the Word of God says about his name.

To discover more about how to use these names in prayer and meditation, you may want to check out *The Prayer Organizer*.[11]

The Law and Commandments

The moral and civil codes of the ancient world were cruel, unjust, and brutal. For example, if someone from another village killed or stole from someone in your village, you could kill the entire village, even though they were not complicit in the crime.

---
11   Dr. Jim Richards, *The Prayer Organizer*, Impact Ministries (

The laws God gave man directly were no different from the Law of Moses. God's laws and commandments were given to show man how to have justice when "meeting out penalties," but also showed man how to avoid crime by walking in love toward one another.

God gave the Ten Commandments as a code of personal morals and ethics at Mount Sinai. Eight of the Ten Commandments were about how to treat others. This is why the Apostle Paul said that when you walk in love, you fulfill the commandments. He wasn't saying that love did away with the commandments; he was saying God's definition of love is based on the Ten Commandments.

When Israel came into the Promised Land, they needed a civil code to maintain peace and order while protecting the innocent from those who would amass political power. Each of the 613 laws of the Civil Code was based on one of the ten original Commandments. They weren't an addition of extra laws. They were an expansion of the Ten into all areas of life and business.

The Law and commandments were never given to make anyone righteous. They were the practical description for walking in love. Those who turned the Law into a method to become righteous misunderstood and misrepresented the Law.

The Law was also a reflection of God's morals, values, ethics, and standards. God had always called the Israelites to be as he was. Therefore, it would be a breach of his honesty to tell them to walk in a moral code that was higher than his personal code. By looking at how he told us to relate to one another, we know exactly how he relates to us. Interestingly, when Jesus taught about the Law, he made it clear that it was not enough to do what the Law said; we should do it from the same motives and intentions as God. If love is not the motive, it changes the entire dynamic of the Law. If harmonizing the hearer with God is not the intention, then we are misrepresenting God! In the Law, we see the core of God's morals, values, standards, and ethics, i.e., his righteousness.

By sorting out how the Law and commandments would be used to express love, we can understand more about God's character and nature.

Immanuel

One of Jesus' names was Immanuel, i.e., God with us! That name is so very suitable, considering if we want to see God as he is, we need to look no further than Jesus! He is God with us! Everything that needs to be known about God can be known through Jesus!

Hebrews 1:1 NKJV says, *"God, who at various times and in various ways spoke in time past to the fathers by the prophets, has in these last days spoken to us by His Son."* In times past, the revelation of God was given through many different sources. But from the time Jesus came to planet Earth, God has not used any other sources to manifest himself to the world.

Hebrews goes on to say, *"Jesus is the exact representation of God."* (Hebrews 1:3) There is no deviation between anything Jesus ever said or did and what God says and does. John 17 reveals the greatest way Jesus glorified God was by being one with him in every word, deed, motive, and intention.

> JESUS' VIEW OF GOD WAS THE ONLY ACCURATE VIEW THAT HAD EVER BEEN PRESENTED ON PLANET EARTH.

Jesus' view of God was the only accurate view that had ever been presented on planet Earth. His sermons, miracles, healings, and ultimately the death he died revealed the character and nature of God. Thus, he declares to the disciples, who were still attempting to know God through the Scriptures alone, *"If you have seen me, you've seen the Father."* In other words, the Scriptures alone will never fully manifest God until we interpret them through Jesus' life, ministry, miracles, death, burial, and resurrection.

Jesus is also called the *"Word made flesh."* (John 1:14) Jesus wasn't just demonstrating the written Word from an intellectual point of view. He showed what God's Word looked like when applied with the Father's motives and intentions. This is what is meant by *the living Word*.

Jesus' life, ministry, teaching, and treatment of people were the first time the world ever saw God clearly. He manifested (made visible) the glory of God. He was not a manifestation of God. He was **the** only accurate manifest of God ever seen by the world! His example reveals God as trustworthy for anyone who's looking. His sacrifice should remove all doubt as to God's good intentions for mankind!

Every interpretation of any Scripture, anywhere in the Bible, must first pass the Jesus test to see if it is in perfect harmony with what we know about Jesus. If our interpretation of Scripture is out of harmony with how Jesus revealed Himself, then we are "off" in our interpretation.

The life-giver

In seeking to understand God, we must identify Jesus' purpose. He said, *"I have come that they may have life, and that they may have it more abundantly.* (John 10:10 NKJV) Everything he did from his birth as a human being, to the life and ministry he presented to the cross where he became our sin, and his death where he bore our punishment, to his final victory through the resurrection was to establish those who would answer the call to be God's family in a perfect life.

If Jesus' every victory was part of the process of obtaining life, then we have to realize that, as far as God's relationship to man, he is always doing what will bring us life to its fullest!

If Jesus came to give us the life of God, the question that begs to be answered is," How does that happen?" We know it doesn't happen automatically upon becoming a believer. We know it can't be earned. It's not even a matter of having enough faith to get it. In John 17:3-4 NKJV, Jesus explains how this transformation takes place. *"… this is eternal life, that they may know You, the only true God, and Jesus Christ whom You have sent."*

The word "know" is the word used to describe the intimacy that is reserved for a husband and wife. It is an intimate sharing where nothing is held back. It is reserved only for the one to whom life-long commitments have been made. It is such a powerful knowing that the Bible says these two people who share this kind of love and intimacy actually become one flesh! Just as Jesus was one with God in motive, truth, purpose, power, intention, love, ad infinitum, in the same manner, we are called to be one with God!

The Bible gives us all kinds of information about God the Father and Jesus, whom He sent! But intellectual information only helps us to know **about** the person. It doesn't actually promote experiential knowledge. Even though you know many things about the person, you still don't know them in that intimate way that forms an eternal bond of oneness.

The New Covenant

Don't confuse the Old Testament and the Old Covenant. Failure to make that distinction causes massive confusion and, for many, becomes the path to self-deception and doctrinal error.

The Old Testament is God's testimony of himself and his interaction with creation and the human race. The Old Covenant is the contract, with all its terms of the agreement whereby man would interact with God. That contract, i.e., the Old Covenant, has been fulfilled and is no longer the basis by which we interact with God!

The New Testament is a record of the testimony of God, with the coming of the Messiah, establishing a New Contract, with new terms, whereby man would interact with God. Both the Old and New Testaments are relevant and crucially important to understanding God. To the degree we abandon the Old Testament, we diminish our understanding of what actually happened in the New Covenant since most of it was planned before the foundations of the earth, set in formation, and explained in the Old Testament. All that information is not only correct; it is vital in understanding the New Covenant.

The New Covenant was not made between all men and God. It was made between God and Jesus. (Galatians 3:15-16) The inheritance that all believers share, was not given to us, the body of Christ. It was given to Jesus, who conquered sin, satan, and death.

In His inheritance, he became the **heir of all things.** If we have joined with him in his death, burial, and resurrection, we are free from the curse of the Law. (Galatians 3:13) Every promise God has made to anyone is yes for us. (2 Corinthians 1:20) We are qualified as heirs, delivered from the power of darkness, and transferred into the Kingdom of his Son. (Colossians 1:20)

To apply any of the conditions of the Old Covenant to our relationship with God is to count as nothing the price Jesus paid for us to have our inheritance in his Kingdom.

The foundations of the faith

The foundation of faith is that upon which we build our spiritual house and establish our hearts! The foundation of any structure is what determines the stability and durability of that which we build.

The foundation provides the boundaries wherein we can seek the most important of all doctrines, righteousness, without stumbling as so many millions have. The writer of Hebrews makes it abundantly clear that without stability in the foundational doctrines, we cannot reach that place of righteousness by faith.

Contrary to pop theology, faith-righteousness is not a process where we use our faith to believe for the gift of righteousness. Righteousness is a gift from God that we receive when we believe the Scriptural version of the Gospel, believe God raised Jesus from the dead, and confess Jesus as Lord. Apart from Lordship, we do not receive righteousness. (Romans 10:9-10)

> CONTRARY TO POP THEOLOGY, FAITH-RIGHTEOUSNESS IS NOT A PROCESS WHERE WE USE OUR FAITH TO BELIEVE FOR THE GIFT OF RIGHTEOUSNESS.

Righteousness is the power that works from our hearts, influences our minds, causes us to see and understand God clearly, and awakens the power of grace, enabling us to live a godly life! (Romans 5:1-2)

The foundations of the faith provide us with six doctrines that help us to not only perceive and walk in righteousness (righteousness being the seventh doctrine) but is the continuum that allows us to see Jesus as he is, thereby knowing and experiencing God.

Without the foundational doctrines, it seems the great majority will twist the doctrine of righteousness, thereby corrupting our perception of God.

The cornerstone

Many believers speak negatively about doctrine as if it is something evil or a waste of time. However, doctrines are based on beliefs. Beliefs determine everything about the quality of our lives. Sadly, many of our doctrines are picked up by default. They come from our culture, tradition, or church affiliation.

The foundations of the faith are made up of the Apostles' doctrine and serve to help us to see God as he is. The medieval church replaced the apostles' doctrine with religious paganism, which led the church and the world into the dark ages. Everything that the world hates about the church has emerged from this doctrinal corruption. The foundations of the faith were based on the Apostles' doctrine, which provided a basis for righteousness, and made it possible to see God as he truly is. Paul said,

> *Now, therefore, you are no longer strangers and foreigners, but fellow citizens with the saints and members of the household of God, 20 having been built on the foundation of the apostles and prophets, Jesus Christ Himself being the chief cornerstone, 21 in whom the whole building, being fitted together, grows into a holy temple in the Lord, 22 in whom you also are being built together for a dwelling place of God in the Spirit.* (Ephesians 2:19-22 NKJV)

There are hundreds of prophetic Scriptures that foretold everything the Messiah would do when he came the first time. It was prophesied that he would die by crucifixion. It gave the exact day he would die and the exact day he would be raised from the dead. They foretold, with incredible precision, the places he would go, the things he would say, and even the miracles he would perform.

The Apostles were Jews. They grew up studying the Scriptures. They knew the Old Testament prophecies about the Messiah. As they watched Jesus minister to the needs of the people, listened to his sermons, and watched his every move, they knew he was the Messiah, based on Scripture. They didn't rely solely on the signs alone.

After Jesus was raised from the dead, the Holy Spirit was poured out, and they understood the Scriptures. They didn't learn about the church and many other important factors because Jesus told them. They saw them in the Scripture. Nearly everything about the church and the New Covenant is revealed in great detail in the Old Testament Scripture. These Scriptures were enlightened by Jesus' teaching.

The Apostle Paul was astounding, as he was able to understand the many facets of what Jesus accomplished by his death, burial, and resurrection through detailed knowledge of the Old Covenant Feasts. They were all types and shadows that revealed what God would do through the Messiah when He appeared.

This is frightening when we consider the effort that has been put forth to encourage believers to abandon the Old Testament Scriptures. Besides the clarity they bring concerning what Jesus has accomplished, they are just as specific about the events surrounding the second coming of the Messiah as they were about his first coming.

As the modern church becomes less knowledgeable about the Old Testament Scriptures, there becomes less of a healthy desire for righteousness. This is reflected in the perverted way people perceive God.

> AS THE MODERN CHURCH BECOMES LESS KNOWLEDGEABLE ABOUT THE OLD TESTAMENT SCRIPTURES, THERE BECOMES LESS OF A HEALTHY DESIRE FOR RIGHTEOUSNESS.

Righteousness is the core of all biblical truth. Without the righteousness of God as the basis of truth, our concepts of love, mercy, grace, and even forgiveness, lose their biblical reality. We hear Christians and ministers promote biblical values, but as it turns out, while they are only saying the same words that are found in the Scripture, they embrace a totally different meaning.

When the apostles make a reference to the Scriptures, they are quoting from what we call the Old Testament. Every New Testament truth is based on the Scriptures as Jesus lived, taught, and modeled them!

Augustine said that the New Testament is in the Old Testament concealed, and the Old Testament is in the New Testament revealed. We need both in order to fully grasp what we have in Jesus, but even more important, we need them both to see God as he is.

Without the Apostles' doctrine, we would never understand how all the pieces of the doctrinal puzzle come together in the person of Jesus. The word of God on the pages of the Bible is just words. There is nothing special about the Bible. But all the Words in the Bible come together to reveal the most unique book ever written. The Bible is filled with prophecies and codes that reveal its consistency and congruence. It is an impossibility that it is the work of mere men.

> EVERYTHING ABOUT JESUS REVEALS EVERYTHING ABOUT THE SCRIPTURE. EVERYTHING ABOUT THE SCRIPTURE MAKES JESUS UNDERSTANDABLE!

But even with all that proof it is the Word of God, it doesn't come to life until it is mixed with faith and is overlayed by the life, teaching, ministry, crucifixion, death, and burial of the Lord Jesus. He is the cornerstone that brings it all together. Everything about Jesus reveals everything about the Scripture. Everything about the Scripture makes Jesus understandable!

Beliefs of the heart

Faith, understanding, wisdom, and every other crucial life concept is rooted in the beliefs of the heart,[3] not the opinions of the mind! Proverbs 17:20 says, *"A crooked heart cannot find good..."* NKJV, & NLT. One of the words that is used to define righteousness is often translated as "straight." So, we have a straight heart that can find good, but a crooked heart cannot.

Proverbs 4: 23 tells us to guard our heart above all else because out of it flows all the issues of our life. The Hebrew says, "Out it flows all the boundaries of our life." Every limitation in our life is based on the boundaries in our hearts, which are created by our beliefs.

The book of Ephesians tells us to put on the breastplate of righteousness. (Ephesians 6:14) In the Old Testament, the priest wore an Ephod, which was basically a vest. Just over the heart was a pocket that contained two stones called the Urim and the Thummim. (Exodus 38:30)

When the nation needed to hear from God, the priest would go before the Lord in a prayerful manner. He would insert his hand into the pocket of His vest to withdraw a stone. Through this process, he could always get yes and no answers concerning the will of God.

The thing that guards and protects our hearts, making it possible for us to always sense the leadership of the Lord, is righteousness. Those who have no commitment to biblical righteousness will always lean toward subjective opinions about God based on personal preferences. They will often not realize the error of their way.

The word of God is compared to light. Light has an interesting characteristic. When it bends, it changes colors. If our heart is crooked, anything we read in the Scripture, or anything God speaks into our heart, will be bent to match the condition and beliefs of our heart. This means no matter how sincere we may be; we will always be off in our understanding of what God is saying!

Here's the dilemma: I can't hear or see God as he is without righteousness in my heart. And I can't have righteousness in my heart until I see and hear him as he is. How can we escape such a dilemma?

It requires a supernatural act of God in our hearts to cross this boundary. When we hear the Gospel, the scriptural account of what happened on the cross, in the grave, and through the resurrection, we have to make decisions and choices. (1 Corinthians 15:1-4)

The first is, do I believe the Scriptural account of the Gospel? Christ died for my sins. But the most important thing we must believe is, did God raise Jesus from the dead, conquering our sin? If I believe that, I must determine if I will trust him as Lord.

The Bible says, "*... with the heart one believes unto righteousness, and with the mouth confession is made unto salvation.*" (Romans 10:10 NKJV) When we believe the Gospel, our heart is transformed. One of the first fruits of being born again is that we start to hunger for righteousness.

Scripture also says that when righteousness comes into our hearts, we are saved, i.e., born again! The state of salvation is the state of righteousness! This is why we immediately begin to realize a shift in our desires.

Confessing Jesus as our Lord is a surrendering of self. It is a choice to follow him and build our lives on his teaching and example. In our hearts, we experience righteousness in more of an intuitive manner. When we study Jesus' life and ministry, we see righteousness put into practice in real life. When we read the Scripture, particularly when we apply the process of Meditative Bible Reading, the Holy Spirit combines what is in our heart, what we see in Jesus' life and ministry, with the scriptures to bring us personal direction and application for the needs in our lives.

As we make this journey, the Foundations of the Faith guard our hearts by renewing our minds to ensure that we do not fall headlong into religious entrapment. The journey becomes easy and light. The more we are transformed into his likeness, the more we love and pursue the righteousness of God through faith in the finished work of Jesus!

For additional information and to locate the resources mentioned in this book please visit:

https://www.truepotentialmedia.com/unshakable/

or use your smartphone camera to open the link in the QR Code below.

Nathan Tanner is an evangelist, author, and humanitarian whose passion to lead people to Jesus has led him to travel to over thirty-five nations on five continents.

Nate and his wife Rute lead L3 International (L3international.org), a global missions movement working in Africa and other places. They regularly see communities transformed by the power of the gospel, and often in some of the worlds most overlooked and forgotten places.

Nate holds a doctoral degree in world evangelism from "Impact International School of Ministry" and has written several books. He has been in ministry since 1998. Nate and his wife have two children and live in Kansas City Missouri.

In 1972, Dr. James B. Richards accepted Christ and answered the call to ministry. His dramatic conversion and passion for helping hurting people launched him onto the streets of Huntsville, Alabama. Early on in his mission to reach teenagers and drug abusers, his ministry quickly grew into a home church that eventually led to the birth of Impact Ministries.

With doctorates in theology, human behavior and alternative medicine, and an honorary doctorate in world evangelism, Jim has received certified training as a detox specialist and drug counselor. His uncompromising, yet positive, approach to the gospel strengthens, instructs and challenges people to new levels of victory, power, and service. Jim's extensive experience in working with substance abuse, codependency, and other social/emotional issues has led him to pioneer effective, creative, Bible-based approaches to ministry that meet the needs of today's world.

Most importantly, Jim believes that people need to be made whole by experiencing God's unconditional love. His messages are simple, practical, and powerful. His passion is to change the way the world sees God so that people can experience a relationship with Him through Jesus.

Jim and his wife, Brenda, have six daughters, 14 grandchildren, and a great-grandchild. They continue to reside in Huntsville, Alabama.

Made in United States
Orlando, FL
16 April 2025